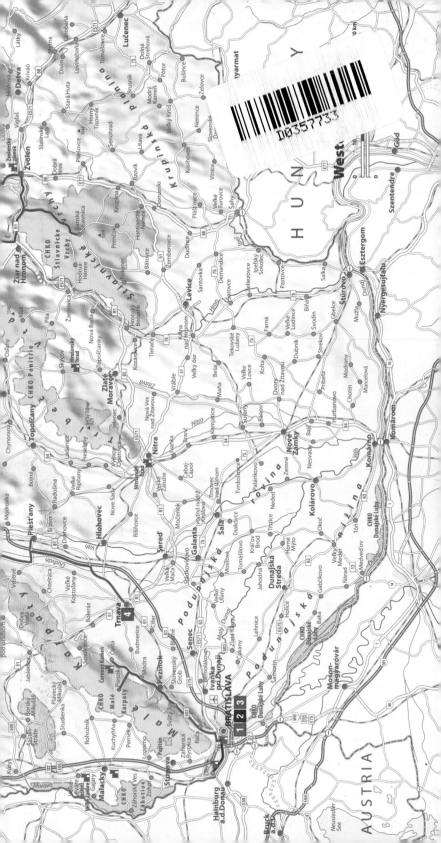

INSIGHT GUIDES

SLOVAKIA
StepbyStep

Windsor _Maidenhead

38067100526190

CONTENTS

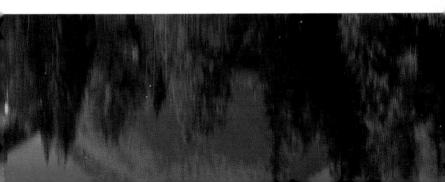

ABOUT THIS BOOK

Above: Slovakian highlights.

This *Step by Step Guide* has been produced by the editors of Insight Guides, whose books have set the standard for visual travel guides since 1970. With top-quality photography and authoritative recommendations, this guidebook brings you the very best of Slovakia in a series of 14 tailor-made tours.

WALKS AND TOURS

The tours in the book provide something to suit all budgets, tastes and trip lengths. They embrace a range of interests, so whether you are an art fan, a keen hiker or have kids to entertain, you will find an option to suit.

We recommend that you read the whole of a tour before setting out. This should help you to familiarise yourself with the route and enable you to plan where to stop for refreshments – options for this are shown in the 'Food and Drink' boxes, recog-nisable by the knife-and-fork sign, on most pages.

For our pick of the walks by theme, consult Recommended Tours For… *(see pp.6–7).*

OVERVIEW

The tours are set in context by this introductory section, giving an overview of the country, plus background information on food and drink, shopping and cultural activities. A brief history timeline highlights the events that have shaped Slovakia over the years.

DIRECTORY

Also supporting the tours is a Directory chapter, comprising a user-friendly A–Z of practical information, our pick of where to stay and select restaurant listings; these eateries complement the more low-key cafés and restaurants that feature within the tours themselves.

The Author

Having taught town planning and landscape architecture for many years, Michael Ivory is now a freelance writer, committed to trying to communicate his enthusiasm for places. Although he has written books on many countries, including Canada and Australia, his speciality is Central Europe. His experience of Slovakia dates back to when the country, still very much part of Czechoslovakia, lay on the wrong side of the Iron Curtain. Western visitors were allowed in, but not exactly encouraged. Visas had to be obtained, routes agreed and accommodation paid for well in advance, and substantial amounts of hard currency exchanged at a distinctly unfavourable rate for every day of the stay. Slovakia turned out to be a revelation, its scenery spectacular, its people friendly, its food filling, its beer as good – almost as good – as that brewed in Bohemia. Since Michael's first visit he has returned many times, revisiting friends, and above all deepening his acquaintance with the country's inexhaustible heritage of unspoiled landscapes and historic towns. What a relief to be able to explore this fascinating country at the heart of Europe free from the tiresome constraints of those early visits! Michael lives in Gloucestershire and in London, where he helps in the work of the British Czech & Slovak Association, a charity devoted to strengthening links between the United Kingdom and Czechoslovakia's two successor republics.

Feature Boxes
Notable topics are highlighted in these special boxes.

Margin Tips
Shopping tips, historical facts, handy hints and information on activities to help visitors make the most of their time in Slovakia.

Key Facts Box
This box gives details of the distance covered on the tour, plus an estimate of how long it should take. It also states where the route starts and finishes, and gives key travel information such as which days are best to do the route, or handy transport tips.

Route Map
Detailed cartography shows the itinerary clearly plotted with numbered dots. For more detailed mapping, see the pull-out map slotted inside the back cover.

Food and Drink
Recommendations of where to stop for refreshment are given in these boxes. The numbers prior to each restaurant/café name link to references in the main text. On city maps, restaurants are plotted.

The € signs at the end of each entry reflect the approximate cost of a main course and glass of house wine for one, with service included. These should be seen as a guide only. Price ranges, also quoted on the inside back flap for easy reference (and in euros for accessibility, although note that the currency in Slovakia is the *koruna*, or crown; SK for short), are as follows:

€€€€   18 euros and above (545SK and above)
€€€   11–18 euros (335–545SK)
€€   7–11 euros (212–335SK)
€   7 euros and below (212SK and below)

Footers
Look here for the tour name, a map reference and the main attraction on the double page.

ANCIENT TOWNS

From Bratislava's Old Town (tour 1) to stately Košice (tour 13), every region has its urban jewels, few quite as perfect as little medieval Bardejov (tour 12).

RECOMMENDED TOURS FOR...

ART LOVERS

Slovakia's towns and cities have the usual complement of museums and galleries with fine collections of painting and sculpture, but the country's outstanding artworks are in the east (tours 10 and 12), where great Gothic churches have an incomparable heritage of medieval carving.

CASTLES

Slovakia's many castles include massive piles stuffed with furnishings, such as Červený Kameň (tour 3) and Krásna Hôrka (tour 14), to spectacular crag-top strongholds including Orava Castle and Strečno Castle (tour 5), to Central Europe's biggest ruin, Spiš Castle (tour 10).

CAVES

Slovakia has numerous cave systems, none more unusual than the ice cave of Dobšina (tour 11), where a kind of underground glacier lurks in the depths.

CHURCH ARCHITECTURE

This Roman Catholic country has well-patronised places of worship from all epochs, though none are more intriguing than the icon-filled Greek Catholic timber churches of the east (tour 12).

FOOD AND WINE

Bratislava is developing into quite a gourmet destination (tour 1), while the Little Carpathian Wine Road (tour 3) takes in not only vineyards and wine merchants but also restaurants specialising in roast goose.

GREAT OUTDOORS

As well as high-level hikes in glorious mountains such as the High Tatras (tours 7 and 8) and the Malá Fatra (tour 5), there is wonderful walking in the ravines of the Slovak Paradise national park (tour 11) and the unique experience of rafting down the River Dunajec (tour 9).

MILITARIA

The epic but little-known struggle of the Slovaks to free themselves from Fascism is commemorated in a unique museum dedicated to the Slovak National Uprising of 1944 (tour 6), while in the east, whole landscapes were marked by the titanic struggle of Wehrmacht and Red Army (tour 12)

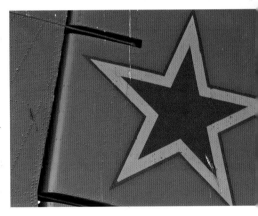

SPAS

Water bubbling up from springs across the country is put to life-enhancing use in spas, from prestigious Piešťany and Trenčianske Teplice (tour 4) to more modest places including Bardejovské kúpele (tour 12) and tiny Štos kúpele (tour 14).

VILLAGES

Much of Slovak life is still lived in the countryside. Well-preserved villages abound, none more perfect than Vlkolínec (tour 5). Traditional rural architecture can also be found in a wealth of open-air museums (tours 5 and 12).

OVERVIEW

An overview of Slovakia's geography, customs and culture, plus illuminating background information on food and drink, shopping, outdoor activities, culture and entertainment, and history.

COUNTRY OVERVIEW

Stunning mountain scenery, evocative spas, towns brimming with historic treasures but not overrun by tourists: Slovakia is a true gem, there to discover for hikers and culture lovers alike.

Overshadowed for centuries by powerful neighbours and more assertive peoples, Slovakia is not only emerging as a self-confident nation but is rapidly acquiring a reputation as one of Europe's most exciting tourist destinations. Small, but far from tiny, it is a country about the same size as Denmark and two-and-a-half times the extent of Wales. It is a mountain country, enfolded in the western extremity of the Carpathians, which

Below: idyllic home in rural Slovakia.

sweep round from the east in a great arc before dropping into the mighty River Danube at the gates of Bratislava, the nation's capital.

CENTRAL LOCATION

Bratislava is situated a mere hour's drive from Vienna, and Slovakia is actually in the heart of Europe; turn up a side road near the town of Kremnica in the central highlands, and you will find yourself at a monument proclaiming the spot to be the geographical centre of the continent.

As well as Austria, neighbours include Poland, Hungary and, bordering the country to the east, Ukraine. The closest ties, however, remain with their fellow-Slavs in the Czech Republic, despite the 'Velvet Divorce' of 1993, when the two peoples failed to agree on a strategy for staying together in Czechoslovakia and went their separate ways. Since 2004, both countries have been members of the European Union (EU).

CAPITAL AND COUNTRY

Capital City
Put firmly on the map by the advent of budget airlines, Bratislava *(see p.28)*, with its beautifully restored, jewel-like

Old Town, is deservedly attracting more and more visitors. As a capital city, it is decidedly off-centre, tucked away in the southwestern corner of the country.

Mountain Country

To the east stretch the broad plains of the Danube valley, but more typical are the Little Carpathians *(see p.38)*; within walking distance of the city centre, these forested uplands are an enticing preview of the rest of the country. It is impossible to go far in Slovakia without the horizon being dominated by mountains, often cloaked to the summits in glorious forests of beech and spruce. The highest peaks, bare of vegetation, are in the High Tatras *(see p.56)*, a short but spectacular range rising sheer from an upland plateau, and a magnet for hikers, mountaineers and winter-sports enthusiasts.

Outdoor Paradise

But though the Tatras top the bill, virtually the whole country is a paradise for lovers of the outdoors, with no fewer than nine national parks as well as countless nature reserves protecting a wonderfully diverse flora – from flower-rich meadows to primeval forests – as well as a teeming fauna, which includes bears, lynxes and wolves. Beneath the surface there are some of the most fascinating cave systems in Europe.

SPAS, TOWNS AND CASTLES

Slovak spas have their own special character. Having long attracted health-seeking visitors, they are fed by abundant natural springs and are often laid out in a sumptuous park-like setting. Piešťany *(see p.42)*, within easy reach of Bratislava, is the most famous, but each region has its watering places.

The country's other towns are frequently surrounded by a rather grim girdle of Communist-era high-rise flats; once beyond these, however, there is usually a well-preserved centre, graced by fine architecture from all eras. Particular concentrations of such fine historic towns are to be found in the Spiš region *(see p.66)* at the foot of the Tatras, and in the centre of the country, whose fabulous medieval prosperity was based on the mining of precious metals.

The Spiš boasts what is claimed to be the biggest castle ruin in Europe, Spišský hrad, but castles, ruined or intact, are to be found everywhere, as well as the country houses *(zámky)* once lived in by Slovakia's privileged Hungarian overlords.

RURAL ROOTS

Half a century ago Slovakia might have qualified for the description 'peasant county', but Communism changed the face of the landscape by a determined policy of industrialisation and urbanisation, planting factories even in the most remote regions. Despite this, rural roots persist, and most town-dwellers retain some sort of connection with the land, visiting village-bound relatives at the weekend or heading to their *chata* (bungalow) in one of the chalet colonies to be seen everywhere.

Above from far left: modern Slovakian; the High Tatras; spectacular forest.

Above: woman in traditional dress.

East and West
Despite its small size, Slovakia exhibits fairly strong regional contrasts. Bratislava and its hinterland is firmly part of bustling Central Europe, looking west to Vienna, Prague and Germany. The east, especially beyond the regional capital of Košice, has affinities with Ukraine, and is noticeably less prosperous.

Castles and Other Grand Domains

The *hrad* in Spišský hrad denotes a castle in the sense of a fortress or stronghold. A *zámok* could also be a castle, but generally denotes something more comfortable like a palace or great country house. Confusingly, a *kaštiel'* is not so much a castle as a manor house or even a big villa.

Below: farming the traditional way.

Traditions and Festivities

And folkways are very much alive; costumes may no longer be part of everyday attire, but are brought out at the slightest excuse, particularly at the many local and regional festivals, and nearly everyone has a repertoire of traditional songs. Slovaks let their hair down on such occasions, though otherwise they may appear rather slow and hesitant in their everyday dealings. This should not be interpreted by the visitor in a negative way; once the first barriers are overcome, these are the most hospitable of people, really going out of their way to make a travelling stranger feel welcome.

MODERN SLOVAKIA

Slovakia is a land to which history *(see p.24)* has not been kind. Somehow retaining its identity despite being incorporated into the Hungarian kingdom for a thousand years, it was very much the junior partner in the former Czechoslovakia. Both experiences left deep resentments. The country's only previous attempt at independence was as a virtual Nazi protectorate between 1939–45 and brought it little glory.

Later, it had a bumpy ride during much of the period of transition from Communism to Western-style democracy, with some authoritarian, scandalridden governments and too many accusations of 'crony capitalism'; at one point in the late 1990s it even seemed unlikely to meet the criteria for Nato and EU membership.

Slovakia Today

Good sense eventually prevailed, leading among other things to one of the more buoyant economies among Europe's post-Communist states. While wages and salaries remain low by Western

European standards, and many young Slovaks are tempted into working abroad, strong educational traditions and a motivated workforce have facilitated a boom in investment: Slovakia is now reckoned to be a world leader in terms of numbers of cars manufactured relative to the size of its population.

Investment is also transforming the country's tourist industry; most of the heritage of standardised Communist-era hotels and restaurants has been brought up to date, and many new facilities added. The country awaits its ever-increasing number of visitors with enthusiasm.

Above from far left: traditionally dressed locals in the Vrátna valley; contemporary architecture in Bratislava; detail of a typical painted wooden cottage; Bratislava rooftops.

Minorities

The great majority of Slovakia's 5½ million inhabitants (86 per cent) are ethnic Slovaks, but there are significant minorities. When Czechoslovakia was created in the aftermath of World War I, ethnic boundaries were ignored in order to give the new state defendable frontiers along the River Danube and elsewhere. A substantial number of Hungarians thereby found themselves detached from the mother country; their descendants today number over half a million, all living along Slovakia's southern border, and determined as ever to maintain their very distinctive Magyar identity. The next largest population group, probably numbering almost as many as the Hungarians, are the Gypsies. Nowadays known by preference as Roma, their marginal way of life was subverted by the Communist regime in a clumsy attempt to integrate them into mainstream society. Their subsequent fate has in many respects been worse; despite constitutional rights and valiant efforts by some members of the community, most Roma suffer every kind of disadvantage, from intolerable housing conditions in isolated slum settlements to poor education, chronic unemployment and low life expectancy.

As you move around northeastern Slovakia you cannot fail to notice signs in Cyrillic script, particularly where village place-names are concerned. These are evidence of Slovakia's Ruthenian (or Rusyn) minority, an ethnic group some 100,000 strong. More Ruthenes, perhaps as many as a million, live in Poland and Ukraine, and something like the same number of Americans can claim a Ruthene ancestor. The most famous of them was Andy Warhol, whose parents emigrated from here in the early 1900s; another was Michael Strank, one of that iconic group of GIs who raised the Stars and Stripes at Iwo Jima in World War II. In Communist Czechoslovakia, Ruthene identity was suppressed; their Greek Catholic churches were closed and their language was replaced by Ukrainian or Slovak. Since the Velvet Revolution *(see p.25)*, however, there has been a great resurgence of Ruthene culture; the language has been revived, the Greek Church has won back much of its property, and summer festivals in centres including Svidník and Bardejov attract substantial crowds.

Famous Slovaks Perhaps the best-known Slovak was Alexander Dubček, who promoted 'Socialism with a human face' during the ill-fated Prague Spring of 1968. Slovak blood flows in the veins of many American citizens, among them Angelina Jolie and Paul Simon.

FOOD AND DRINK

The Slovak kitchen produces solid, simple but tasty dishes and mouth-watering cakes and pancakes – a heritage from its links with Hungary. This overview explains where to sample it and what to look for on the menu.

Traditional Slovak food is hearty and straightforward, based on the products won with some difficulty from the mountain and forest environment and intended to sustain hard-working lives in harsh circumstances.

There are dairy products such as sour milk and sheep's cheese, potatoes, rye bread, and noodles, dumplings and pasta of various kinds. The king of vegetables is the cabbage, the most prized animal the pig. With much in common with Czech food, this basic diet is made a little more exotic by the Hungarian influence, with paprika playing an important role, and goulash featuring on most menus.

Nearly every eating place in the country serves this kind of food; it is a genuine national cuisine with its own integrity, and is surprisingly well balanced, provided that those consuming it adopt lifestyles to counter the effects of excess calories. It should certainly

Below: friendly sign for meals at a local *pension*.

be tried, though there is no lack of alternatives; recent years have seen a dramatic increase in the number and variety of restaurants and in the range of international dishes served. Bratislava in particular has eating places that pander to seemingly every palate.

WHERE TO EAT

As well as the conventional restaurant (*reštaurácia*), eating establishments in Slovakia include: wine cellars (*vináreň*), which are broadly similar but may stay open longer and offer a wider choice of wine; pubs (*piváreň*); and, perhaps more interestingly, rustic places called either *koliba* or *salaš*. Variations on the traditional shepherd's hut, both types of establishment specialise in food and drink drawn from the traditional repertoire. The usual range of fast-food establishments abounds, with local specialities dispensed from a *bufet* (buffet).

BREAKFAST

When it is eaten at home, breakfast (*raňajky*) is a simple meal of bread and butter with ham, cold sausage, cheese, and jam or honey, plus possibly some fruit or yoghurt. Coffee – of which all the usual types are available – is generally preferred to tea, which is invariably weak and may be fruit- or herb-based.

Most hotels serve a more elaborate version of this, usually presented in buffet form, and often with a warm dish such as scrambled eggs.

LUNCH AND DINNER

The main meals of the day, lunch (*obed*) and dinner (*večera*), are eaten rather earlier than is the custom in Western Europe, and are essentially similar, though most local people confine themselves to a cold meal in the evening if they have eaten substantially at midday.

Starters and Soup

Starters (*predjedla*) are usually dispensed with in favour of a nourishing soup (*polievka*); favourites include garlic, chicken and cabbage soups, the last of the three often enlivened with mushrooms, tasty morsels of meat or sausage, and topped with cream.

Meat Dishes

The central part of the menu will be dominated by meat dishes, the majority of them based on pork, followed by chicken, though beef,

Mladé víno Malaga

Svätovavrinecké 2006

Above: local honey; Slovak wine.

National Dish

Slovaks' favourite meal goes under the name of *bryndzové halušky*. *Bryndza* is sheep's cheese, melted and poured over the *halušky*, dumplings made from potato dough and bearing a close resemblance to Italian gnocchi. This rather stodgy ensemble is perked up by having fried bacon dice scattered liberally over its surface and is traditionally accompanied by a beaker of *acidofilné mlieko* or *zakysanka*, a delicious cross between sour milk and runny yoghurt.

Mushrooms

With the right climatic and other conditions, Slovakia supports thousands of mushroom species, which are picked with passion by the locals. Considerable expertise is necessary to distinguish the edible from the poisonous. Visitors lacking the time or knowledge to go mushroom-hunting should watch out for roadside vendors selling them instead.

Below: scrumptious Slovakian strudels.

veal and turkey are also likely to feature. Lamb is relatively rare, and not liked by most locals, and when served in expensive restaurants it may well have been imported from New Zealand. Roast goose is a special treat, and Slovakian game of all kinds is well worth trying.

Fish

Ocean fish is uncommon, often only appearing as anonymous-sounding *filet*, but freshwater fish can be excellent; as well as trout, there is delicious pike-perch or zander, while carp is bred in quantity as the centrepiece of the Christmas Eve dinner, filleted, breadcrumbed and fried.

Vegetables and Pasta

The main dish is usually accompanied by a garnish, but other vegetables will need to be ordered separately, if required. Slovak potatoes are usually good, and are best eaten boiled or roasted rather than as chips. Green vegetables are less common than salads, though broccoli may appear on the menu. Vegetarians do better nowadays than in the past, when all that was on offer was an omelette or fried cheese (the latter tastier than it sounds); most of the better restaurants offer at least a limited range of meatless options.

Pasta dishes are popular, *bryndzové halušky* most of all *(see p.15)*, but also ravioli-like *pirohy*.

SWEETS

Desserts may be passed over altogether in favour of a separate session at some point in the day at the patisserie *(cukráreň)*, with its tempting display of tasty and surprisingly light cakes and pastries. But ice cream will always be on the menu, and a pancake *(palacinka)*, filled with cream and fruit and lashings of chocolate sauce, is virtually a meal in itself.

DRINK

Beer

Like their Czech neighbours, Slovaks are extremely fond of beer *(pivo)*, and the country produces a number of very respectable brews as well as importing some of the better-known Czech brands. Among the most popular beers available are Zlatý bažant (Golden Pheasant), Smädný mních (Thirsty Monk) and Šariš, served either on draught or bottled.

Wine

However, Slovakia is also a wine *(víno)* country, with extensive vineyards all along its sunny southern border with Hungary. Even part of the famous Hungarian Tokay vineyards are on Slovak territory. Communist-era insistence on quantity above all else has given way to an increasing concern with quality; Slovak wines are well worth trying and are invariably better value than expensive imports. Slovakian whites are generally superior to the reds.

Spirits

Among local spirits, fruit-based brandies including *slivovica* (plum brandy) can be excellent, especially if locally made and matured, while gin-like *borovička*, flavoured with juniper berries, is worth sampling.

Water and Soft Drinks

As a land of springs and spas, Slovakia is awash with mineral waters, all of them able to make some special contribution to your health and all worth sampling. Ask for the local *mineralka*, especially if you are in or near a spa. International soft drinks are available everywhere, but many locals still prefer *kofola*, the local cola.

SHOPPING

These days anything can be bought in Slovakia, but it is the handcrafted folk-art objects, incredibly varied in design and materials, that make the most interesting souvenirs, as well as perhaps a bottle of plum brandy.

Above: carved wooden figures; sign at a crafts stall; woven basket; decorative bucket.

The days are long since gone when queues lined up patiently in front of Communist-era shops with distinctly un-enticing window displays beneath a fascia labelled 'Meat' or 'Shoes'. Retailing is one of the economy's most dynamic sectors; malls and superstores – some less aesthetically pleasing than others – seem to have shot up at breakneck speed, particularly in some of the outskirts of the capital, Bratislava. As a result, everyone, including the visitor from abroad, can find more or less everything they want, provided they can afford it.

It should, however, be noted that price levels in such places are hardly different from those anywhere else in Europe, and in some instances may even be higher.

WHERE TO SHOP

Town centres tend to be dominated by smaller, individual shops and boutiques, which generally makes for a pleasant shopping experience. That said, a stroll around a Slovak supermarket can give you insight into what the locals buy, and most such places have a good selection of local food and drink, with well-stocked delicatessen counters and shelf upon shelf of wines and spirits.

SOUVENIRS

Until about the mid-20th century most Slovaks lived on the land. Folk traditions, crafts and costumes were still very much a matter of everyday life, with great differences in style between the country's regions. Like everything else, folkways were subjected to centralised direction under Communism, but at least were kept alive. Since the 1990s there has been a revival of individual craft production, and the visitor will find plenty of fascinating and unusual items to purchase.

Traditional craft objects can be viewed and purchased in the chain of shops run by ULUV (Centre for Folk Art Production), which has branches in a number of places as well as Bratislava. Dielo shops deal more in contemporary arts and crafts. Traditional items can also be found at the numerous folk festivals and in the open-air museums known as *skanzens*. It is also worth investigating antique shops *(starožitnosti)*, of which there is one at least in towns of any size.

Pottery and Woodwork

Pottery and ceramics include painted plates, jugs, vases, flasks, tiles and even statuettes. Elaborately perforated plates are particularly attractive. The

majolica produced in the small town of Modra near Bratislava is much admired, with its blue-and-yellow floral patterns and depictions of seasonal work in farm or vineyard. More pervasive than pottery are objects made of wood, of which there is no shortage in Slovakia. These range from simple implements such as cooking spoons and forks and shepherd's cups and bowls to figurines, patterned moulds for cakes and cheeses, and beautifully carved serving dishes.

Seasonal Decorations

Traditional Slovakian Christmas decorations come in many different natural materials, and are a welcome alternative to the usual shiny, over-finished baubles and other objects. Figures for the Christmas crib can be charming. Decorated Easter eggs are marvels of meticulous pattern-making, using a variety of techniques, from etching to batik.

Other Handmade Crafts

Tinker products have a long tradition in Slovakia, and unusual filigree-like objects fashioned from wire can occasionally be found. Basket-work comes in all sorts of shapes and sizes, while pretty corn dollies *(see picture, right)* are made of dried maize leaves. Painting on glass, which once concentrated on religious motifs, now applies its colourful technique to various themes, with Jánošík, the Slovak Robin Hood *(see p.46),* as a popular subject.

Attractive rugs, blankets, embroidery and delicate lacework can all be found, as can items of traditional clothing. However, perhaps the most unusual souvenir would be a *fujara,* a very long shepherd's pipe, which resembles a didgeridoo and emits, with practice, a not dissimilar noise.

Above from far left: colourful Modra pottery; traditionally embroidered skirt.

Below: corn dollies.

OUTDOOR ACTIVITIES

With a largely unspoiled countryside, suitably dramatic mountains and glorious forests, Slovakia is in many ways an ideal destination for people drawn to the great outdoors.

Out Hunting

Given the country's rich wildlife, hunting is something of a cult in Slovakia, with its own rituals and appropriate apparel. Rabbits and wildfowl can be pursued almost everywhere, and larger prey like deer and boar are abundant. Even bears and wolves can sometimes be shot.

Slovakia is very much a sport-minded nation, making an impact out of all proportion to its size in football (soccer), tennis and, above all, ice hockey. Its people make the most of its mountainous terrain, treading the thousands of kilometres of marked paths in summer, scaling cliff and rock the year round, and flocking to more than 100 ski centres in winter. Rivers, lakes, vast reservoirs, thermal pools and conventional swimming pools stand in for the missing seaside.

For more practical information on various outdoor activities, log on to the following sites: www.travelslovakia.sk, www.slovakia.travel or www.sacr.sk.

HIKING, CLIMBING AND CYCLING

A dense network of meticulously way-marked paths and trails facilitates hiking. The most spectacular scenery is in the High Tatras, made all the more accessible by the existence of high-level resorts, a network of funiculars, chairlifts and cableways, and well-located mountain huts and chalets. But all the mountain ranges are worth exploring, particularly those like the Low Tatras and Great and Little Fatras, where long-distance ridge-walks of several days are possible.

Rock climbing has many devotees, not least because in the High Tatras some of the most challenging climbs are far more easily reached than in the Alps. Even ordinary hikers can make it to some of the highest peaks, such as Gerlach (2,499m/8,198ft), though many summits are only accessible in the company of a guide.

Cycling is also big; as well as its footpaths, Slovakia has the beginnings of a national network of cycleways, with more than 5,000km (3,107 miles) of roads and trails signposted by the Slovak Cycling Club. An increasingly popular route, beginning in Germany and ending at Budapest, is the trail along the Danube, which in Slovakia connects Bratislava with the town of Komarno. A more challenging itinerary with plenty of ups and downs leads through the Spiš region between the Dunajec gorge and the ancient town of Levoča, while several national parks have routes set aside for mountain bikers.

ON THE WATER

A novel way of experiencing some of the country's most spectacular landscapes is aboard a raft. Traditionally costumed rafters pole their passengers along stretches of the rivers Váh and Hron, but the most dramatic trip is

through the deep gorge of the River Dunajec in the Pieniny national park.

A more conventional way of exploring these and other rivers is by canoe, while yachtsmen, windsurfers and waterskiers are catered for on the broad waters of the many reservoirs, of which the 22-sq-km (8.5-sq-mile) Liptovská Mara in the centre of the country is the largest. There is an artificial wild-water channel here, and another at Čunovo, a short distance down the Danube from Bratislava.

Rivers and lakes offer abundant opportunities for fishing, the main species being trout, eel, pike, tench and catfish. Permits can be obtained locally, often from the tourist information centre.

SKIING

With its normally guaranteed snowfall, this mountainous country really comes into its own in winter, when seemingly the whole population straps on skis or snowboards. There are more than 100 skiing centres, with a variety of runs which overall cater for every level of proficiency. Most centres have invested in new and improved facilities such as lifts and snow-making equipment, and modernisation continues.

Among the most important skiing areas are the High Tatras, where the snow lies longest, Jasná and Donovaly in the Low Tatras, Velká Rača Oščadnica in the Beskydy mountains, and Vrátna and Ružomberok in the Fatras. Congestion at peak times can be a problem, and après-ski attractions do not yet match those of the Alps. Against this, board and lodging, passes and hire of equipment are inexpensive.

Cross-country skiing is practised everywhere, even in towns, while a more challenging development for the adventurous is alpine touring, which requires special equipment and should not be undertaken lightly.

Above from far left: rock climber in Sulov; spectacular country for snowsports; cycling is popular in Slovakia.

Below: extreme mountain climbing.

CULTURAL ACTIVITIES

There is a thriving cultural scene in Slovakia, and its accessibility to the non-Slovak visitor is good thanks to a proliferation of musical performances, ballet and puppet theatre, plus a wide number of films screened in English and other foreign languages; the comparatively inexpensive prices are a bonus too.

Cultural life in Slovakia is vibrant, particularly in the capital city Bratislava *(see p.28)* and the second city – dubbed the 'Jewel of the East' – Košice *(see p.82)*, with their array of opera houses, concert venues, theatres, cinemas and other places of entertainment. Other major towns all have their theatres and concert halls hosting a variety of events year-round, though note that some stop for a summer recess.

THEATRE, OPERA AND CLASSICAL MUSIC

Slovak National Theatre

Austrian culture vultures from nearby Vienna are not above sneaking down the River Danube to Bratislava in order to hear fine opera and classical music at the city's Slovak National Theatre (Hviezdoslavovo námestie 1; tel: 02 5443 3083; www.snd.sk; *see p.29*), where tickets cost a fraction of the price they pay at home. The season runs from September to June. Note that operas usually have surtitles in Slovak or German, so it's advisable to read up on the plot beforehand, if you are unfamiliar with it. Ballet is also performed here, as are plays, although these may be rather less accessible to most tourists, as they will be in Slovak.

Puppet Theatre

An excellent option for non-Slovak-speakers, especially those with children, is a puppet show. The best place to see one of these in Bratislava is at the Puppet Theatre (Dunajská 36; tel: 02 5292 3668; www.babkovedivadlo.sk). Here, versions of fairy-tales and other endearing stories have been re-enacted using carved and painted wooden puppets – and some modern ones – since 1957.

Classical Music

There has long been a thriving classical-music scene in Bratislava, perhaps not surprising given its proximity to Vienna. In 1762 Mozart gave a performance at the Palffy Palace *(see p.31)* at the tender age of six, while older musicians to set foot in then-Pressburg *(see p.31)* include Haydn, Liszt, Bartók and Beethoven, whose *Missa Solemnis* premièred in Bratislava. In terms of home-grown talent, the country's most eminent composer is Johann Nepomuk Hummel (1778–1837), who wrote mostly for the piano.

Nowadays, the country's main orchestra is the Slovak Philharmonic (Slovenský filharmónie), which performs in the historic Reduta building (Palackého 2; tel: 02 5443 3351/2;

Bratislava Film Festival
Film mania hits the Slovak capital every year, at the end of November/start of December, in the shape of the International Bratislava Film Festival (www.iffbratislava.sk). Established in 1999, the festival sees around 50 screenings per day across the city and awards to Slovak and foreign films. If you're interested in Slovak cinema, directors' names to look out for include Juraj Jakubisko (b.1938), Dušan Rapoš (b.1953), Ivan Reitman (b.1946) and Martin Šulík (b.1962).

www.filharmonie.sk). Tickets are available online at www.ticketportal. sk. Chamber-music concerts and recitals are often held in the Primate's Palace *(see p.31)* and the 18th-century Rococo Mirbach Palace *(see p.33)*.

Roma Theatre

Košice is home to the Romanthan, a venue devoted to the promotion of Roma theatre, music and other cultural events and the only state-funded one of its kind in Europe.

OTHER NIGHTLIFE

For other forms of nightlife, there is nowhere to touch Bratislava with its array of bars, clubs and performance spaces catering to the huge student population. DJs play the latest international and local hits, and the city

hosts live concerts by a surprising number of international stars.

FILM

English-language films are often presented in the original version with Slovak subtitles, making a trip to the cinema a feasible option for visitors from the UK and US. 'ST' is code for 'with Slovak subtitles' and 'CT' stands for 'with Czech subtitles'; however, 'SD' means that the film has been dubbed in Slovak, and 'ČD' that it has been dubbed in Czech. Arthouse cinemas include Filmový Klub (Imricha Karvaša 2, Bratislava; tel: 02 5296 1712; www. nostalgia.sk); see the website for the current programme (in Slovak but discernible, as film names are in the original). Movie buffs may like to visit for the International Film Festival *(see left)*.

Above from far left: Slovak National Theatre; folk dancing; Mirbach Palace.

Folk Dancing
There is a strong tradition of folk dancing in Slovakia. Slovakian restaurants often put on displays of traditional dancing or host what are known as 'dance houses' (tanečný dom), a mix of performance and dance class. See www.tanecnydom.sk for more information.

Below: Bibiana (www.bibiana.sk) is an organisation promoting culture in Slovakia, with its focus on literature for children; it also mounts art exhibitions.

HISTORY: KEY DATES

There are many chapters in the Slovak history books. Key periods include the Great Moravian Empire; Hungarian, Ottoman and Habsburg rule; the establishment of the new state of Czechoslovakia; the fall of Communism; and, finally, independent rule and membership of Nato and the EU.

EARLY PERIOD AND GREAT MORAVIAN EMPIRE

5th–1stC BC	The territory of Slovakia is inhabited by Celts.
1st–2ndC AD	Southwestern Slovakia is disputed between Germanic tribes and the Roman Empire, whose frontier runs along the Danube.
AD 179	The legions of Emperor Marcus Aurelius march into Slovakia as far as Trenčín in pursuit of the Germanic Markomans.
400s	Slovakia colonised from the east by Slavs, who are the ancestors of today's Slovaks.
623–58	The Frankish merchant Samo places himself at the head of 'Samo's Realm', a confederation of western Slav peoples.
833	Consisting of Moravia and western Slovakia, the 'Great Moravian Empire' is founded by Prince Mojmír.
863	Cyril and Methodius, the 'Apostles of the Slavs', promote Christianity in the Great Moravian Empire.
896	The nomadic and heathen Hungarians arrive in the Danube lands, defeating a Bavarian army sent against them at the Battle of Bratislava (907).

HUNGARIANS, OTTOMANS AND HABSBURGS

Scottish Slovakophile
Few Britons are honoured with a monument in Slovakia. The Scot R.W. Seton-Watson (1879–1951) is an exception; his promotion of Slovak independence from Hungary is marked by a plaque in the central Slovak town of Ružomberok.

1000	Foundation of the Hungarian kingdom under the Christian King Stephen I. The Slovaks are fated to live under Hungarian domination until the early 20th century, their country referred to as the 'Felvidék' (the 'Highlands' or 'Upper Hungary').
1241–2	After devastation wrought by Tatar hordes, German colonists are invited in by the Hungarian kings to repopulate parts of Slovakia.
1526	The Turks annihilate the Hungarian army at the Battle of Mohács. After their subsequent occupation of most of Hungary, the capital of the Hungarian kingdom (now ruled by the Habsburg dynasty) is transferred to Bratislava.
16th–early 18th century	Led by Protestant Hungarian noblemen, a series of rebellions against Catholic Habsburg rule take place on Slovak territory.

SLOVAK AWAKENING

1800s	Growing awareness of Slovak national identity.
1848–9	The 'Year of Revolutions'. Slovaks side with Habsburg forces in the face of strident Hungarian nationalism.
1863	The 'Memorandum of the Slovak Nation', demanding recognition of Slovak rights, is ignored by the Hungarian authorities, who institute a rigorous programme of Magyarisation.

TWO WORLD WARS AND COMMUNISM

1918	As the Austro-Hungarian Empire crumbles at the end of World War I, Slovaks join with Czechs in founding Czechoslovakia. The new state is multi-ethnic, democratic, but highly centralised; the Prague government fails to grant Slovakia its promised autonomy.
1939	Under pressure from Nazi Germany, Slovakia secedes from Czechoslovakia and forms the nominally independent 'Slovak State', its leader the Catholic priest Father Tiso.
1941	Slovak forces cooperate with Germany in invading the Soviet Union, and Slovakia declares war on Britain and the US.
1944	Defeat of the Slovak National Uprising and occupation of the country by German forces.
1945–7	After liberation by the Soviet army, Czechoslovakia is re-established as a centralised state. Expulsion of Sudeten Germans, the Slovak German minority, and part of the Hungarian minority. Father Tiso executed as a traitor.
1948	Communist coup d'état and introduction of totalitarian rule.
1968	Led by Slovak politician Alexander Dubček, the 'Prague Spring', an attempt to introduce 'Socialism with a human face', is crushed by Soviet tanks. Federalisation is the only reform to survive, but despite the creation of a Slovak parliament, all major decisions are still made in Prague.

POST-COMMUNIST PERIOD

1989	The 'Velvet Revolution', with centres in Prague and Bratislava, brings about the fall of Communism.
1993	Unable to agree on how to live together in Czechoslovakia, Czechs and Slovaks separate in the 'Velvet Divorce'.
2004	Slovakia joins Nato and the European Union (EU).
2009	Slovakia adopts the Euro.

Above from far left: coloured, engraved map of Bratislava by the artist Joris Hoefnagel (1542–1600), reproduced from *Civitates Orbis Terrarum* by Georg Braun (1541–1622) and Frans Hogenberg (1535–90); German and Russian tanks locked in combat in the so-called Valley of Death (due to the number of World War II battles held in the area), Svidník; Alexander Dubček, speaking in 1969.

WALKS AND TOURS

BRATISLAVA

A tour exploring Slovakia's capital city. Begin with a stroll through the picturesque streets and squares of the Staré mesto (Old Town), followed by a mildly strenuous climb up to the formidable bulk of Bratislava Castle. Consider pairing this tour with the trip to Devín Castle (see p.36).

Student City
With several universities and other institutions and a student population of 65,000, Bratislava may be an ancient place but has a decidedly youthful air and lively atmosphere.

Below: Bratislava rooftops.

> **DISTANCE** 3.5km (2 miles)
> **TIME** Half a day
> **START** National Theatre
> **END** Bratislava Castle
> **POINTS TO NOTE**
> Nearly the whole of Bratislava's compact Old Town is pedestrianised, making walking a pleasure. But city streets can be hard on the feet, especially when there are steps and steep ramps to be negotiated. Comfortable, stout footwear is highly recommended for this tour.

Bratislava exerts a magnetic pull on Slovaks as well as on visitors from abroad. Though relatively small as a capital city by international standards, with 450,000 inhabitants, it is far and away the country's biggest city, well linked to the rest of prosperous Central Europe by road, rail and air. Only around 60km (37 miles) down the Danube from Vienna, its size, location and dynamism make it attractive to business as well as to tourism, and its economy has developed rapidly since the fall of Communism, drawing migrants in from the rest of the country, as well as a substantial influx of foreigners.

History of the City

A century ago, Bratislava (known then by its German name of Pressburg), was a modest-sized provincial town, still largely contained within the line of its demolished fortifications, its population consisting mostly of Germans and Hungarians, a substantial Jewish community, but only a small number of Slovaks. The formation of the new state of Czechoslovakia in 1918 from the ruins of Austria-Hungary boosted the Slovak element, though it was only after World War II that the city took on an overwhelmingly Slovak char-

acter. No fewer than a third of today's inhabitants live on the south bank of the Danube in the endless high-rise blocks of the Petržalka district; no contrast could be greater than that between the soullessness of this monument to Communist housing policy and the intimate charm of the Old Town, its inviting streets lined with the Baroque residences of a long-gone aristocracy.

NATIONAL THEATRE

Begin your tour at the lovely Ganymede Fountain located in front of the **Slovak National Theatre ❶**

(Slovenské národné divadlo); the theatre was built in Renaissance-cum-Baroque style in 1886 by the ubiquitous Viennese duo of Fellner and Helmer, responsible for theatres and opera houses all over Austria-Hungary. The theatre stands at one end of **Hviezdoslavovo námestie**, the attractive, tree-lined square (or rather boulevard) named after Pavel Országh Hviezdoslav, the 'Father of Slovak Poetry', whose statue graces the centre of the square.

Head towards the Danube along Mostová ulica, passing between the square's other dominant structures; to

Above from far left:
Bratislava Castle;
atmospheric
passageway in
the Old Town.

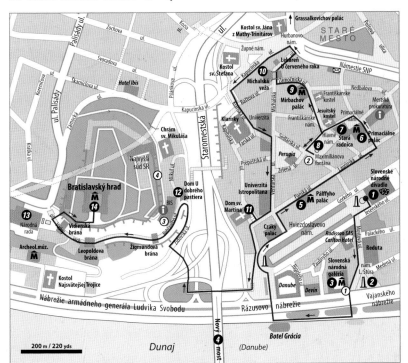

Coronation Hill

More of a low mound than a hill, this artificial eminence would be ascended by the newly crowned monarch, who would brandish his (or her) sword towards all four points of the compass, a token of his (or her) determination to defend the realm against all comers.

Below: a stroll through the Old Town.

the left is the Reduta, home of the Slovak Philharmonic, to the right, the monster Carlton Hotel. Facing the river, **Ľudovít Štúr Square** (Námestie Ľudovíta Štúra) was once the site of the so-called Coronation Hill *(see left)*.

THE DANUBE

Use the pedestrian crossing over the busy riverside highway for a close-up view of the powerfully flowing waters of the mighty Danube and its proces-

sion of barges and pleasure steamers, and perhaps for a pause in the appropriately named **Café Propelor**, see ①①, housed in a little Functionalist building from the 1930s.

Slovak National Gallery

On the landward side of the embankment is the **Slovak National Gallery** ③ (Slovenská národná galeria; Tue–Sun 10am–5.30pm; charge), housed in a Baroque barracks, whose appearance was not enhanced in Communist times by the notably brutalist wing facing the Danube.

Highlights of the collections include exquisite Gothic sculpture from the Spiš area of eastern Slovakia as well as fascinating examples of the Slovak contribution to 20th-century art and design. The gallery also hosts temporary exhibitions.

A possibly more successful Communist-era addition to the scene is the **New Bridge** ④ (Nový most), a spectacular piece of engineering supported by angled pylons topped by a UFO-shaped panoramic restaurant *(see p.116)*.

INTO THE OLD TOWN

Leave the riverside by the modern Hotel Danube and walk inland to the west end of Hviezdoslavovo námestie, where a Baroque Trinity column commemorates Bratislava's deliverance from an outbreak of plague in 1713.

Aristocratic Palaces

Turn right into the square and walk along the north side past a droll statue

---

Food and Drink

① CAFÉ PROPELOR

Rázusovo nábrežie 1; tel: 02 5400 1020; €

A fine example of interwar architecture, the riverside Propelor (meaning 'steamer') offers outdoor dining and drinking with an unsurpassed view over the Danube.

of the Danish writer Hans Christian Andersen (1805–75), who spent some time in Bratislava and described it as a fairy-tale city.

Now turn left, then right into **Panská** ('Lord Street'), which owes its name to the many aristocratic palaces along its length. One of the finest, the Baroque **Palffy Palace ❺** (Pálffyho palác; Tue–Sun 11am–6pm; charge), houses artworks from the city's collections.

A less than aristocratic note is struck by the corner of Panská and Rybárska brána by an amusing and eye-catching pair of bronze sculptures; one is a helmeted figure apparently emerging from underground, the other, just up the street to the left, is based on 'Schöner Náci', the nickname of a Bratislava character of pre-war days *(see right)*. Similarly quirky statues appear throughout the Old Town.

Primate's Palace

Continue along Panská ulica, turning left into Uršulínska, the street named after the Ursuline church and monastery at its end. Uršulínska leads into Primaciálne námestie, a spacious square dominated by the pink façade of the **Primate's Palace ❻** (Primaciálne palác; Tue–Sun 10am–5pm; charge). Built in 1781 for Cardinal Battyányi, Primate of Hungary, this monumental, neoclassical structure boasts a Hall of Mirrors and fabulous 17th-century tapestries woven in the Royal Manufactory in England's Mortlake.

Old Town Hall

A passageway gives access to the charming arcaded courtyard of the **Old Town Hall ❼** (Stará radnica; Tue–Fri 10am–5pm, Sat–Sun 11am–6pm; charge). A harmonious combina-

Schöner Náci
Given his mockingly German moniker (short for Ignaz/ Ignatius), 'Handsome Náci' was a real-life eccentric of Old Bratislava. Despite being more or less destitute, Náci dressed up every day in tails and topper before strolling the city streets, a bunch of flowers in hand ready to present to any lady that took his fancy. Nowadays his shiny statue makes an amiable companion for tourists having their photograph taken.

What's in a Name?

Bratislava has been known under various names in the past. Its German name is Pressburg, and for centuries German-speakers formed a majority of its inhabitants. But by the 12th century, as part of the Hungarian kingdom, it had acquired its official Magyar name of Pozsony. Until the 20th century, Czechs and Slovaks called it Prešporok, their version of Pressburg. The trio of names symbolised the more or less harmonious coexistence within the city of the different communities, but with the foundation of Czechoslovakia after World War I, the need was felt for a name of appropriately Slavonic character. Scholars came up with 'Bratislava', a word with a number of advantages: a) it had nothing German or Hungarian about it; b) it was reminiscent of the medieval Slav prince Brazlav; and c) it had satisfactory overtones of brotherhood or brotherly love (*brat* in the Slavonic languages means 'brother'). Nevertheless, despite banishment for the best part of a century, the name 'Pressburg' has enjoyed a recent revival, and is used in a nostalgic way to evoke the 'good old days' of the Austro-Hungarian Empire.

Town Hall Bell

In 1733, the master bell-founder Johann Ernst Christelly was ordered to cast a fine bronze bell to grace the Town Hall. Jealous of his wife's dalliance with the city's lord mayor, he took the opportunity of thrusting his rival into the vat of molten metal. All that is left of the unfortunate mayor is the diamond from his ring, supposedly responsible for the bell's sweet tone when rung.

Below: arcaded courtyard at the Old Town Hall.

tion of architectural styles ranging from Gothic onwards, the Old Town Hall now belongs to the City Museum, whose varied collections tend to be upstaged by the historic interiors in which they are displayed.

AROUND THE MAIN SQUARE

Go through the vaulted passageway into **Hlavné námestie 8**, Bratislava's main square, on the far side of which stands the 16th-century **Maximilian Fountain** (Maximiliánova fontána). The fountain's statue, representing either Emperor Maximilian or the knight Roland, is said to revolve on his perch every New Year's Eve; however, this phenomenon is apparently only visible to virgins. Almost always bustling with activity, the square is the

city's most popular meeting-place, a favourite rendez-vous being **Café U Rolanda**, see ⑪②, on the ground floor of no. 5, a fine example of Art Nouveau architecture by the Hungarian architect Ödön Lechner.

Jesuit Church

Walk back across the square towards **Františkánske námestie** (Franciscans' Square), on the way noting the statue of the Frenchman in a three-cornered hat leaning on a bench, another much-photographed scene. Next to the Old Town Hall is the sober structure of the **Jesuit Church** (Jesuitský kostel). Built by the city's Lutheran community in the early 17th century, it was forbidden by the Catholic authorities to have a tower, and was soon confiscated and given to the Jesuits, who fitted out the interior in characteristically exuberant

Baroque style. Outside the church, topped by a figure of the Virgin Mary, stands one of the many columns erected all over the Habsburg Empire to mark the triumph of the Counter-Reformation over Protestantism.

Mirbach Palace

Facing the Franciscan Church at the far end of the square is Bratislava's finest Rococo-style palace, the **Mirbach Palace ❾** (Mirbachov palác; Tue–Sun 11am–6pm; charge), gorgeously decorated inside and out, and used mostly by the city art gallery for temporary exhibitions.

AROUND MICHAEL'S TOWER

The narrow lane **Zámočnicka** curves round to the left, bringing you into one of the Old Town's most attractive streets, **Michalská ulica**. Together with its continuation southwards **Ventúrska ulica**, it has been colonised by cafés, restaurants and a scattering of upmarket shops, and buzzes with life, particularly on summer evenings when you may find it difficult to find a seat.

Featuring in every picture-book on Bratislava is **Michael's Tower ❿** (Michalská veža; Tue–Sun 10am–5pm; charge). This splendid medieval tower with its Baroque cap, together with the barbican beyond, is the most impressive remnant of the city's fortifications; it is now the home of a small museum devoted to weaponry, but the real reason for paying the modest entrance fee is to enjoy the fine view

over the Old Town from the top.

Just through the gate is the **Red Lobster Pharmacy** (Lekáreň U červeného raka), complete with its fine old-fashioned sign. Beyond the barbican, the city moat, long since dry, is crossed by a bridge. On the right, marking the transition to the relatively modern, more spacious part of the Old Town, is a prime example of the Functionalist architecture of interwar Czechoslovakia, the boxy Baťa shoe shop, now a fashion store.

From here, the broad boulevard of **Námestie SNP** runs downhill; its name honours the Slovak National Uprising of 1944 *(see p.52)*. It is one of the city's main commercial arteries, as well as a forum for gatherings and demonstrations.

Straight ahead and just about visible some 500m (547yds) away is the delicate grey-and-white Rococo façade of the **Grassalkovitch Palace (**Grassalkovichov palác), the official residence of the President, guarded by smartly dressed soldiers in traditional uniform.

The University

Turn left towards the castle on its hilltop and follow the tramlines for

Above from far left: Old Town Hall bell tower; Art Nouveau detail at Café U Rolanda; Red Lobster Pharmacy; Grassalkovitch Palace.

Little Blue Church
A striking Art Nouveau building by the architect Ödön Lechner is the fantastical, extravagantly ornamented Little Blue Church (Modrý kostolík), tucked away on Bezručova ulica to the east of the Old Town. Completed in 1913, it is dedicated to St Elizabeth, one of Central Europe's most loved saints, who died in 1231 at the tender age of 24 having devoted her short life to the care of the sick, poor and elderly.

Food and Drink 🍴

② CAFÉ U ROLANDA
Hlavné námestie 5;
tel: 02 5443 1372; €
Enjoy the urban scene from the outdoor terrace right by the Roland statue, or sample tasty cakes in the high-ceilinged interior of this gracious establishment.

Petržalka
If it was an independent city, this vast housing estate, shown above, would be the third-largest town in Slovakia. Built from the 1970s onwards to accommodate Bratislava's explosive growth in the Communist era, it is made up of what Slovaks call *paneláks*, high-rise structures built from concrete panels mass-produced on site.

Bratislava's Jews
Before World War II, around 10 per cent of Bratislava's population were Jews. The wartime puppet regime was strongly anti-Semitic in character, and actually paid the Nazis to deport the country's Jewish population. But popular outrage was such that the deportations were halted, and only resumed during the German occupation in the last months of the war.

about 200m (656ft), turning left again down a flight of steps which brings you into Klariská ulica and a tranquil part of the Old Town, likely to stay that way as most buildings – some unrestored – are owned by the Church.

At this point walk down Klariská and return to the hubbub of Michalská through a passageway to the left, and continue into Ventúrska ulica. The lively atmosphere here is partly due to the presence of the **Univerzitá Istropolitana**, the city's most venerable university, originally founded in the mid-15th century.

ST MARTIN'S CATHEDRAL

You will recognise the junction of Ventúrska with Panskà from earlier in your walk; here you turn right, then right

Food and Drink 🍴

③ MODRÁ HVIEZDA
Beblavého ulica 14;
tel: 02 5443 2747; €€
Conveniently located on the lane climbing up to the castle, the 'Blue Star', with its atmospheric brick vaulted cellar cut into the hillside, offers Austrian, Hungarian and Slovak specialities.

④ HRADNÁ VINÁREŇ
Nám. A. Dubčeka 1;
tel: 02 5934 1358; €€€
The best place to take a break after climbing up to the castle is in this establishment on the eastern side of the precinct, less for the food and drink, though these are adequate, than for the superlative view over the Old Town.

again up steps to the **St Martin's Cathedral** ⓫ (Dom sv. Martina), the city's most important place of worship, whose doorway is on the far side. With Budapest under Turkish occupation for centuries, St Martin's served as the coronation church for no fewer than 19 Hungarian monarchs, among them Empress Maria Theresa. Inside, St Martin is honoured by a monumental equestrian statue in lead by the esteemed Austrian Baroque sculptor Georg Rafael Donner, who was also responsible for the sumptuous decoration of the side chapel of sv. Jan Almužník.

THE SYNAGOGUE

Go back down the stairway to the south of the cathedral and turn right, passing the old pharmacy at no. 35, whose inscriptions in German, Hungarian and Slovak are a reminder of the city's former multicultural character. In front of you is the site of Bratislava's main synagogue, where a Holocaust memorial now stands, bearing the Hebrew word 'Zachor' ('Remember'). The synagogue itself is depicted on the Wall of Memory to the west.

TOWARDS THE CASTLE

Make your way beneath the spaghetti junction at the city end of the New Bridge and go right up a flight of steps. You are in what was once one of the city's most fascinating quarters, a warren of narrow streets and picturesque houses, nearly all of which were demolished to make way for the

approach to the bridge. A few fragments remain, among them the **Good Shepherd House** ⓬ (Dom U dobrého pastiera; May–Sept: Tue–Fri 10am–5pm, Sat–Sun 11am–6pm, Oct–Apr: Tue–Sun 9.30am–4pm; charge), a pretty corner building in Rococo style housing a wonderful collection of clocks and other timepieces.

A Steep Climb

You now need to take a deep breath and begin your climb up the castle hill. (Modrá Hviezda, see ⓘ③, is just nearby, if you need fortification.) The steep lane first winds past a number of venerable buildings up to the richly decorated Gothic gateway known as the **Sigmund Gate** (Žigmundová brána).

While you can continue through the gateway, a less strenuous approach to the castle leads off to the left, running below the fortifications to the modern buildings of the **Národná rada** ⓭, the country's Parliament. At the top of the slope, turn right through the **Vienna Gate** (Vidienská brána) and walk with the crowds who have come up the easy way in their tourist buses.

Bratislava Castle

You now enter the forecourt of **Bratislava Castle** ⓮ (Bratislavský hrad; Tue–Sun 9am–5pm; charge). With its plain walls almost bereft of any form of ornament and its four corner towers, the castle has been unflatteringly compared to an inverted table or bedstead.

Its present severe and homogeneous appearance belies its complicated past;

it has been built, rebuilt and added to many times, sometimes as a fortress, at other times as a palace. In 1811 a fire started by drunken soldiery reduced it to a shell, and it was only during Communist times that it was restored to provide reception rooms for state occasions and accommodation for several departments of the National Museum. These feature period furniture, silverware and a museum of music, though the prize exhibit is the so-called *Venus of Moravany*, a female fertility figure carved some 23,000 years ago from mammoth bone.

You can also climb the Crown Tower and enjoy a superb panorama over Bratislava and its surroundings. However, the view from the broad terrace in front of the castle is hardly less spectacular, despite being dominated by the sight of the apartment blocks of the Petržalka estate marching relentlessly into the distance. For more views and a bite to eat, try the **Hradná vináreň**, see ⓘ④.

GETTING BACK DOWN

You can return to the Old Town by trolleybus from a stop below the Vienna Gate or by descending the steps leading to the Sigmund Gate and returning the way you came. A pleasant alternative is to walk round the eastern side of the castle, turning right down steps through the outer defences and finding your way down to Židovská ulica past the little **St Nicholas's Church** (Chrám sv. Mikuláše).

Above from far left: the castle at night; view over the Old Town from the castle; sign at the Good Shepherd House; detail of the Holocaust memorial, reading 'Remember'.

Above: details of 19th-century stained-glass windows in St Martin's Cathedral.

DEVÍN CASTLE

This trip involves a short bus ride to Bratislava's hilltop fortress at Devín, overlooking the confluence of the River Morava and the River Danube. Consider doing this tour in afternoon, having walked route 1 in the morning.

DISTANCE 15km (9 miles) return
TIME Half a day
START/END New Bridge (Nový most), Bratislava
POINTS TO NOTE

This excursion involves either a return bus journey or an outward bus journey and a return steamer trip. If you are taking the bus both ways, buy tickets for both the outward and return journeys from the kiosk at the Nový most bus station in Bratislava and stamp them on entering the bus. If you are interested in returning to Bratislava by boat, note that the service can be infrequent, so check as you arrive in Devín or in advance on tel: 02 5293 2226. There is usually a departure towards the end of the afternoon.

Food and Drink

① HRADNÁ BRÁNA

Slovanské nábrežie 15 Devín; tel: 02 6010 2511; €€€

The most comfortable place to relax and refresh yourself after visiting Devín castle is this four-star hotel located right by the castle entrance. It has a restaurant serving traditional Slovak dishes as well as international cuisine, but also a more informal café and outdoor terrace.

The Virgin's Tower
This is the name given to the slim little tower perched precariously on a rock pillar high above the Danube on the castle cliff. Legend has it that it was from here that a noble maiden jumped to her death when her husband, the knight Nicholas, was assassinated only days after their wedding.

The Devín rock has been occupied by every group of people that has ever attempted to control this key location. Among them were Late Stone Age peoples, Celts, Romans, Hungarians and Germans. During the Great Moravian Empire, distant ancestors of today's Slovaks sallied forth from here to win a couple of famous victories over their adversaries.

The Middle Ages to the Present

The castle was first mentioned in writing in 864. After that the fortifications were improved and altered over the centuries. The castle's present ruined state is due to Napoleon's troops, who most disrespectfully blew it up when they passed this way in 1809.

Later in the 19th century it became a great symbol of Slovak nationhood; its distinctive silhouette is instantly recognisable to even the least patriotic inhabitant, and nationalist rallies are held here as well as outdoor summer performances of various kinds.

TOWARDS DEVÍN

Buses nos 28 and 29 leave Bratislava from the northern end of the New Bridge (Nový most, *see p.30*). Alight at the first stop in Devín (marked 'Základná škola').

Along the River Bank

From the bus stop, walk back down the road for a short distance, then turn right along a side road which eventually runs along the banks of the Danube, past the steamer landing stages towards the confluence with the River Morava. This whole area was forbidden frontier territory in Communist times, and there is a memorial to those who died trying to flee Communist Czechoslovakia by swimming the river to the Austrian bank.

THE CASTLE

Continue along the pathway into a large car park and turn right into **Devín Castle** (Hrad Devín; May–Sept: Tue–Fri 10am–5pm, Sat–Sun 10am–7pm, Apr, Oct–Nov: Tue–Sun 10am–5pm; charge). Devín has everything a castle ruin should have: a crag-top location commanding the rivers below, extensive ramparts, several gateways, towers and bastions, to say nothing of legends and a real history of extraordinary length and incident. It is quite a climb through the well-preserved ruins to the highest point of the castle, but well worth it

for the view over the surrounding landscape and the contrastingly coloured waters of the Danube (bluish-grey) and Morava (brown).

Options for refreshment at the castle include the restaurant or café of the **Hotel Hradná brána**, see ⑪①.

THE RETURN TRIP

To return to Bratislava, you can either take bus no. 29, which departs from outside the castle, or no. 28 from the village main street. For an alternative approach, take the steamer from the landing stage that you passed after getting off the bus. The trip takes only 30 minutes, but service is infrequent *(see grey box, left)*.

Above: Devín Castle's exterior walls.

Below: Devín Castle and the Danube.

3

LITTLE CARPATHIAN WINE ROAD

A tour through the vineyards extending northeastwards from Bratislava along the foot of the Little Carpathian mountains, visiting lovely old wine towns and villages and ending at the historic hilltop castle of Červený Kameň.

DISTANCE 76km (47 miles) return
TIME At least half a day
START/END Bratislava
POINTS TO NOTE

All the places on this tour are easily reached by public transport, but taking your own car allows more flexibility.

Fugger Finance
The south German Fugger family grew rich thanks to their ownership of the medieval metal mines of central Slovakia, which in the 16th century were producing nearly 3 tons of silver a year, to say nothing of vast quantities of copper. At the height of their wealth and power the Fuggers could make or break emperors and were bankers to the Vatican.

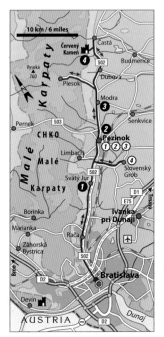

Drive northeast out of Bratislava city centre along Mýtna and Račianska streets in the direction of Pezinok. Even before you have reached the city limits on main road no. 502, vineyards begin to clad the lower slopes of the Little Carpathians (Malé Karpaty).

SVÄTÝ JUR

A short distance further on, and the vines almost completely surround the little old town of **Svätý Jur ❶** (St George). Wine has been made here since time immemorial, and the town still has a number of traditional single-storey vintners' houses with high-roofed cellars. On the slopes above stands a castle, left in ruins after a Turkish assault in 1663. In the parish church is Svätý Jur's greatest treasure, a 16th-century altar sculpture, hewn from a single block of stone, of St George calmly sticking the dragon.

PEZINOK

The next wine town, **Pezinok ❷**, is larger, with a rectangular square and stately buildings including an early 17th-century vintner's house, now the seat of the **Museum of the Little**

Carpathians (Malokarpatské Múzeum; Mar–Nov: Tue–Fri 9am–noon, 1–5pm, Sat 9am–3pm, Sun 1–5pm; charge), which deals very thoroughly with the area's viticulture and local history. There are plenty of places to sample and purchase the local wines, an activity perhaps best postponed until you are on your way back to Bratislava *(see Food and Drink box, p.40).*

MODRA

Just 8km (5 miles) further on, **Modra** ❸ is celebrated by Slovaks for its associations with one of their great national heroes, the 19th-century patriot Ľudovít Štúr (1815–56). As well as for wine, the little town is famous for its ceramics.

Developed originally by a community of Anabaptists, religious refugees from Switzerland and Moravia, Modra folk majolica features delightfully fresh floral patterns in blue and yellow.

ČERVENÝ KAMEŇ

From Modra, a minor road leads up into the hills, ending at the recreational centre of **Piesok**, the starting point for hikes to summits such as Skalnatá and Vysoká offering panoramic views over the mountains. The main road leads through the villages of Dubová then Častá, where signs direct you up through the Carpathian woodlands to your final destination, the hilltop stronghold of **Červený Kameň** ❹

Above from far left: wine country; Anton Fugger's 16th-century cellars.

Modra Pottery
A good place to investigate Modra ware *(illustrated left)* is Miroslav Malinovksý (Štúrova 60; tel: 0903 796 474), a pottery on the main square, where you can usually see the owner at work and purchase items for considerably less than in Bratislava.

Above from left:
Slovakian grapes; the
River Váh, near Trenčin.

Carpathian Wines

The lower slopes of
the Little Carpathians
provide excellent
conditions for the
production of wine.
With a variety of
suitable soils, they
face southeast
towards the sun-
drenched plains of
the Danube, and are
protected to the north
by the well-wooded
mountains. While
Bratislava itself boasts
the greatest area of
vineyards, those
of Svätý Jur are
supposed to be the
best, those of
Pezinok the prettiest
and those of Modra
the most productive.

Food and Drink 🍴

① MESTSKÁ VINOTÉKA
Radničné námestie 9, Pezinok;
tel: 033 641 1132; wine only
Run by an amiable lady expert, this
ancient establishment – the 'Town
Wine Cellar' – makes an atmospheric setting in which to sample
carefully selected vintages from the
Little Carpathian region and from
other parts of Slovakia. No food.

② VINO MATYŠÁK
Holubyho. 85, Pezinok; tel: 033 641
3667; €€
An unpretentious restaurant run by a
local vintner as part of his centuries-
old winery, where you can enjoy your
hearty lunch or supper with vintages
drawn from the barrel.

③ ZÁMOCKÁ VINÁREŇ
Pezinok Castle, Mladoboleslavská 5,
Pezinok; tel: 033 641 2360; €€–€€€
With a history going back to the 13th
century, Pezinok's castle is now the
headquarters of the area's largest
winery, with a choice of atmospheric
interiors in which to sample the best
of the region's food and drink.

④ GROBSKÝ DVOR
Vajnorská 3, Slovenský Grob;
tel: 033 647 8889; €€€€–€€€€€
A short distance off the main road
no. 502 between Svätý Jur and
Pezinok, at the entrance to the village of Slovenský Grob, this family
restaurant prides itself on serving
some of Slovakia's most succulent
roast goose.

(daily 9am–5pm; charge). The castle's
origins go back to the Middle Ages,
when it was one of a chain of fortifications along the border between the
Czech kingdom and Hungary.

It was subsequently associated with
several of the most eminent names
in the history of Slovakia, including
the aristocratic Thurzo and Pálffy
families and also the Fugger mining
dynasty. The Fuggers *(see p.38)*
constructed cavernous underground
works that were originally intended for
the storage of copper, but which in the
end were only ever used as wine cellars.

More recently the splendid fortress
has provided settings for Fantasy films,
including *Dragonheart* (1996), and pop
concerts. There is plenty to see in the
rest of the castle, from arms and
armour to fine period furnishings in a
variety of interiors, and in season all
kinds of outdoor entertainments are
organised, from historical pageants to
displays of falconry.

GOOSE AND WINE

Return to Bratislava the way you came,
perhaps stopping for a wine-tasting
in Pezinok, followed by dinner in one
of the town's restaurants. Recommendations include **Mestská Vinotéka**,
Vino Matyšák and **Zámocká Vináreň**, see 🍴①, 🍴② and 🍴③.

Alternatively, turn left off the main
road 3km (2 miles) south of Pezinok
to **Slovenský Grob**. The fame of this
village was based on the geese raised
here, then done to a turn on stone
ovens and supplied to Bratislava gourmets. Nowadays the gourmets drive
out to the village, to enjoy their goose
in one of a number of specialist
restaurants, such as Grobský Dvor,
see 🍴④.

ALONG THE VÁH

This tour takes you along the valley of Slovakia's longest river, the Váh, introducing some of the traditional spas, historic towns and impressive castles so characteristic of the country.

TRNAVA

Often referred to as the 'Slovak Rome', the city of **Trnava ❶** is dominated by its churches. For centuries, following the rout of the Hungarian army by the Turks in 1526, it was the most important ecclesiastical centre in Hungary, and in 1635 one of its archbishops founded one of the first universities on Slovak territory. But as the Turks were driven out of the kingdom, and important institutions were claimed back by Budapest, Trnava, like Bratislava, lost most of its former importance, and quietly mouldered away. Even Communist attempts to convert it into an industrial town failed to stop it becoming something of a mellow backwater. To take in its atmosphere, stop off at **Hotel Barbakan**, see ⑪①.

DISTANCE 98km (60 miles)
TIME A full day
START Trnava
END Trenčianske Teplice
POINTS TO NOTE
Use of your own car would be a distinct advantage when doing this route, though most of the places visited are accessible by public transport. Start at Trnava, 50km (31 miles) from Bratislava by motorway D1/E50 and finish at the spa town of Trenčianske Teplice.

Above: university church of St John the Baptist; Thermia Palace Hotel.

Food and Drink 🍴

① **HOTEL BARBAKAN**
Štefánikova 11, Trnava; tel: 033 551 4022; €€€
Pleasant town centre hotel with a café, cellar pub and restaurant offering dishes of the day as well as à la carte and regional specialities. The pub incorporates a microbrewery which, amazingly, turns out a stout as well as the usual light beers. Outdoor seating in the courtyard in summer.

Left: the twin towers of St Nicholas Cathedral.

Above from left:
water-lily at the luxury
Thermia Palace Hotel;
gateway into the ruins
at Čachtice; portrait
of Elizabeth Bathory.

'Get Up and Go!'
Piešťany's symbol
of a naked man
breaking his crutch
over his knee *(shown
above, top)* is a vivid
expression of the
healing properties of
the town's waters.
The 'crutch breaker'
features in the town's
coat of arms and,
more famously, in the
bronze figure *(shown
above, bottom)* by
the bridge over the
Váh, a work of 1933
by the sculptor
Robert Kühmayer.

As well as extensive remains of fortifications, the town has imposing
civic buildings, including an Empire-
style theatre, built in 1831 and the

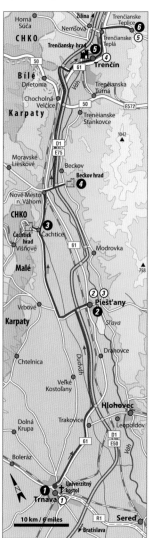

first of its kind in Slovakia. Of its
churches, the most striking is not
so much the cathedral as the **Uni-
verzitný kostol**, the imposing twin-
towered university church. One of the
country's largest Baroque places of
worship, it boasts a sumptuously stuc-
coed interior and an extraordinarily
lofty altarpiece.

PIEŠŤANY

From Trnava's ring road, drive northeast on road no. 61, turning right after
10km (6 miles) in the village of
Trakovice and joining the D1/E50
motorway towards **Piešťany** ❷.
This internationally famous spa town
glories in hot springs, which with
their high gypsum and sulphur con-
tent have been known since early
medieval times. In the past, the waters
were drunk by popes and emperors,
but today's clientele is largely drawn
from the Middle East and the lands
of the former Soviet Union.

Spa Facilities

The town does its best to provide a
relaxing environment for its guests,
with lavish parks and gardens laid out
along the banks of the Váh. The main
facilities are located on an extensive
island in the river, approached by a
colonnaded bridge, which features
a well-known sculpture of a patient
celebrating his cure by smashing his
crutch. On the far river bank, setting
the tone of the spa, is the **Thermia
Palace**, a splendid relic of the Art
Nouveau era with a sumptuous inte-

rior. Among the town's restaurants are the **Hotel Pavla**, see ⑪②, and **Le Griffon**, see ⑪③.

ČACHTICE

Leave Piešťany to the west, crossing over the motorway and continuing towards Nové Mesto nad Váhom on road no. 504. Remain on this road for 13km (8 miles) as far as the centre of the village of **Čachtice ❸**, notorious for its associations with the 'Blood Countess' Elizabeth Bathory.

The Castle

There is a small and not particularly enthralling museum in the village, while the site of Elizabeth's outrages, **Čachtice Castle** (Čachtický hrad; May–Oct: Wed–Sun 9am–5pm; admission charge), can be reached from the village by a steady climb on foot (about 40 minutes) or by driving 6km (4 miles) along the minor road towards Višňové, parking and setting off on a much steeper but shorter climb. There is not much evidence of the bloody countess among the gaunt ruins, but the view over the surrounding hills and valleys is particularly fine.

TRENČÍN

Return to the main road and pass through the town of Nové Mesto nad Váhom, following the signs to Trenčín and Žilina and rejoining the motorway. Look out for another spectacular crag-top ruin to the right, the remains of **Beckov Castle ❹** (Beckovský

hrad). Leave the motorway at the second exit signposted Trenčín, follow signs to Centrum and turn right into one of the car parks at the approach to the town centre.

Of the many medieval castles along the course of the Váh, the town of **Trenčín ❺** has the most formidable, **Trenčín Castle** (Trenčiansky hrad; daily, May–Sept: 9am–5.30pm, Oct–Apr: 9am–4pm; charge), a towered stronghold rising over an extravagantly fortified rocky outcrop. At the turn of the 13th and 14th centuries it was the headquarters of a near-legendary figure, the magnate Matúš Čák *(see p.44)*.

Roman Remnant

With an historic core reached through a medieval gateway, the town of Trenčín is pleasant enough; it boasts

---

Food and Drink 🍴

② HOTEL PAVLA
Sad Andreja Kmeťa 76,
Piešťany; tel: 033 774 3091; €€
Built in the 1920s in crisp, functional style, the Pavla has been thoroughly refurbished. As well as an attractive café with a view of the river and the spa island, there is a coolly contemporary restaurant with a wide choice of modern international as well as Slovak cuisine.

③ LE GRIFFON
Winterova 29, Piešťany; tel: 033 774 1903; €–€€
Established nearly two centuries ago, and named after one of Piešťany's springs, the popular Griffon provides conventional dishes, as well as fare with something of the flavour of Provence.

Elizabeth Bathory
A member of one of Hungary's great aristocratic families, Elizabeth gained her notoriety through her taste for the blood of young girls. Helped by her lesbian lover, she is thought to have been responsible for the deaths of some 600 unfortunates, and was only brought to justice when she broke an unwritten rule and began torturing and killing young noblewomen instead of mere servants and peasants. Elizabeth was walled up in Čachtice Castle, but her ghastly career and fate were kept secret lest disgrace be brought on the family name.

Matúš Čák

Styling himself 'Lord of the Váh and Tatra', this colourful figure defied the Pope as well as the kings of Bohemia and Hungary. His successful rule over much of present-day Slovakia fore-shadowed the independence so long denied the country, and earned him a popularity among patriotic Slovaks that has lasted to this day.

Below: Trenčín.

a unique curiosity, a Latin inscription carved into the rock face beneath the castle by the soldiers of Roman Emperor Marcus Aurelius, who ventured here, far beyond the Empire's Danube boundary, in pursuit of the troublesome Germanic tribesmen in AD 179.

Places to eat in Trenčín include the restaurant of the **Hotel Tatra**, see ⑪④.

TRENČIANSKE TEPLICE

From Trenčín, continue for another 9km (5 miles) along main road no. 507, turning right in Trenčianska Teplá to **Trenčianske Teplice** ❻. Attractively laid out along a wooded valley, this is one of the most appealing of Slovak spa towns, its centrepiece a gorgeous mock-Moorish bathhouse, the **Hammam** (open for spa treatments and to other visitors only Mon 3.30pm; charge) built in 1888. Equally fascinating, though far more sober in style, is the open-air swimming complex called **Zelená Žába** (Green Frog), a fine example of the progressive architecture of interwar Czechoslovakia. As in all Slovak spas, there is a good range of places to stay. A good pitstop for lunch is **Dedinka**, see ⑪⑤.

Food and Drink ⑪

④ HOTEL TATRA

Ul. Gen. M R Štefánika 2, Trenčín; tel: 032 650 6111; www.hotel-tatra.sk; €€–€€€
One of those Slovak institutions traditionally serving as the town's chief meeting-place, the century-old Tatra has a choice of gourmet dining in the main restaurant, rustic specialities in its Slovenska *reštauracia*, and coffee, cakes and light meals in the Café Sissi. It also offers a close-up view of Trenčín's famous Latin inscription.

⑤ DEDINKA

Kupelná 13, Trenčianské Teplice; tel: 032 655 1476; €–€€
Push past the unimposing door to this restaurant in the middle of the spa area and you find yourself in the unlikely setting of a Slovak village, with doors opening off into rustic rooms. Traditional country cuisine – and piped folk music – to match food of a definitely superior standard. Specialities include Pacho's Balls and Highwayman's Golden Coins.

MALÁ FATRA MOUNTAINS

A drive around the first high mountains on the road linking Bratislava with the rest of the country. From Žilina, the busy regional capital, the tour penetrates the most spectacular part of the range, then continues past castles, historical towns and the deep wooded gorge of the meandering Váh.

ŽILINA

Life in **Žilina ❶**, reached from Bratislava in just over two hours by express train or by car via motorway D1/E50, revolves around elegant **Mariánske námestie**, the arcaded square that forms the focal point of the city's medieval core, high above the more modern town at its foot. The square is a good place to get your bearings and something of the feel of this busy regional centre, whose history goes back to its foundation in the early 14th century by German settlers. Medieval prosperity gave way to a long

DISTANCE 175km (108 miles)
TIME One or two days
START/END Žilina
POINTS TO NOTE

This itinerary is only practicable by car. To enjoy a ramble in the mountains you will need to stay overnight and bring your walking shoes and water-proofs. There is a reasonable selection of places to stay, particularly in the tourist centre of Terchová, where as well as a number of modern, small or medium-sized hotels there is an abundance of pensions and chalets.

Above from far left: Trenčín Castle; interior *(left)* and exterior *(right)* of the Moorish bath-house in Trenčíanske Teplice; spectacular Malá Fatra mountains.

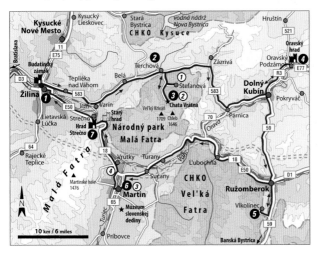

Mayoral Mischief
Despite his ultra-right Slovak National Party forming part of the ruling coalition government elected in 2006, its leading light Jan Slóta failed to obtain a ministerial post. For many years he governed Žilina as its ever-newsworthy mayor, notorious for his drunken benders, coarse language, threats to invade Hungary and set up concentration camps for Slovakia's Roma.

period of decline brought about by plague, pestilence and fire, and the town only regained prominence when it became an important railway junction in the late 19th century. It was, and still is, one of the strongholds of Slovak nationalism, evidence of which can be seen in the **Námestie Andreja Hlinku**, the vast square in the lower town. Overlooked by the bell tower of the big parish church, and linked to the upper town by an imposing ramp and stairway, the square is named after the priest and politician Andrej Hlinka (1864–1938) whose statue is a prominent feature here *(see box p.49)*.

Budatín Castle
Žilina has a number of museums, but the only one of exceptional interest is housed on the town's northern outskirts in **Budatín Castle** (Budatínský zámok; Tue–Sun, June–Aug: 8am–5pm, Sept–May: 8am–4pm; charge). Of several exhibitions in this round-towered castle on the far bank of the

Váh, the most fascinating is devoted to the work of local tinkers, whose sheer artistry in wire often beggars belief.

TERCHOVÁ

At this point, follow signs from the town centre towards Čadca and then Terchová. Main road no. 583 runs eastwards towards the Malá Fatra massif, and after 28km (17 miles) reaches the popular tourist resort of **Terchová ❷** on the northern flank of the range.

Burned down towards the end of World War II, this sprawling village offers its many guests a range of accommodation, from three-star hotels to bed-and-breakfast establishments in private houses. It is famous for its summer folk festival and even more so as the birthplace of Juraj Jánošík (1688–1713) – the Slovak equivalent of the English folkloric figure Robin Hood – whose glittering metallic statue stands high above the village *(see below)*.

Slovakia's Robin Hood

A native of Terchová, Juraj Jánošík (1688–1713) took part in an anti-Habsburg rebellion, then fled to the hills, where he turned to banditry. Whether or not he really followed the example of English folkloric hero Robin Hood in robbing the rich to pay the poor, he soon became a thorn in the side of the authorities. After only a year or so of this activity, he was betrayed by an innkeeper, tortured and put horribly to death, hanged from a hook thrust into his rib-cage. His brief period of freedom, his selflessness and his sad fate continue to appeal to Slovaks, who have immortalised him in word, song and film.

VRÁTNA VALLEY

After paying tribute to this most popular of Slovak folk heroes, head south along the road through the Vrátna valley that penetrates into the heart of the mountains. Beyond the jagged limestone crags of the narrow Tiesňavy defile, a side road to the left leads to the village of Štefanová, where you can eat at **Pension Muráň**, see ⑪①.

The main route continues past a skiing area to **Chata Vrátna ❸**, the chalet at the foot of **Veľký Kriváň**, at 1,709m (5,607ft) the highest summit in the range. A modern cable-car whisks visitors to a height of 1,500m (4,921ft), just below the adjoining summit of **Chleb** (1,646m/5,400ft), from where there are fabulous panoramic views.

Hiking Country

Hiking possibilities are endless here; European long-distance trail E3 threads its way along the ridge, giving access to the distinctive pointed summit of Veľký Rozsutec to the east as well as to various side paths dropping back down to Chata Vrátna. Some of the most fascinating treks in the range are along the deep and narrow defiles cut by streams into the limestone rocks. Once you are hungry, head for **Slovenská Koliba – Hotel Diery**, see ⑪②.

ORAVSKÝ HRAD

Go back to Terchová, turning right to continue eastwards on road no. 583, then left again on road no. 70 after 26km (16 miles) towards the district town of Dolný Kubín. Continue north for 9km (5 miles) on road no. 59 and be amazed at the sight of Slovakia's most spectacularly sited stronghold.

The Castle

Added to in every conceivable style since its foundation in the 13th century, **Orava Castle ❹** (Oravský hrad; Tue–Sun, May–June and Sept–Oct: 8.30am–5pm, July–Aug: 8.30am–6pm, restricted hours rest of year; charge) perches precariously on a rocky spur rising precipitously from the banks of the rushing River Orava. From its seemingly impregnable walls, the region's Hungarian rulers could resist incursions into their kingdom from the north and command the important trade route into Poland.

The castle now houses a local museum, featuring peasant costumes

Food and Drink 🍴

① PENSION MURÁŇ
Štefanová 554, Terchová;
tel: 0903 737 057/041 562 0788; €
Straightforward meals and snacks served in a cheerful mountain pension at the upper end of the charming village of Štefanová, with a cosy dining room and a veranda. Much favoured by serious walkers and mountaineers as a place to stay.

② SLOVENSKÁ KOLIBA – HOTEL DIERY
Biely Potok; tel: 041 569 5322; €
This hotel at one of the entrances to the Vrátna canyon walks has built itself a convincingly authentic *koliba*, where you can enjoy equally authentic traditional dishes at remarkably reasonable prices.

Above from far left: ladder up a *Diery* route *(see below)*; memorial to Joraj Jánošík; rustic *koliba* window.

Walks with a Difference
The attractive mountain village of Štefanová is the starting point for challenging walks along a trio of *Diery*. Literally meaning 'caverns', they are so called because they originated when the roofs of underground streams collapsed, forming narrow gorges. The streams and their frequent waterfalls have been made accessible by means of ladders and catwalks, which are great fun if you are reasonably agile, have a head for heights and do not mind the occasional soaking.

Above from left:
traditional farming
methods; painting by
Martin Benku at the
museum in Martin.

Choosing a Capital
Martin's central
location and the
presence here of
important institutions
made it a serious
candidate for the role
of Slovak capital when
Czechoslovakia was
founded in 1918. An
additional advantage
was its purely Slovak
character, compared
with multicultural
Bratislava, dominated
at the time by its
German and Hun-
garian inhabitants. But
hardly bigger than a
village, and lost
among its mountains,
little Martin simply
seemed too far away
from the action, and
Bratislava it had to be.

and stuffed bears, but more gripping
than the collections are the picturesque
courtyards, gateways and ramparts, to
say nothing of the giddy views down
to the river, 100m (328ft) below.

Return to Dolný Kubín and drive
south on road no. 59/E77 through the
industrial town of Ružomberok.

VLKOLÍNEC

Still on road no. 59 in the direction of
Banská Bystrica, look out for a sign
4km (2.4 miles) to the south of the
town pointing right to **Vlkolínec ⑤**.
The narrow lane twisting its way up
the mountainside was only made
accessible to cars in the 1990s,
bringing to an end the isolation which
had spared the village from all forms
of modernisation and left it in a state
of perfect preservation. No cars are
permitted in Vlkolínec, and as well as

<table>
<tr><td colspan="2">Food and Drink 🍴</td></tr>
<tr><td colspan="2">③ PASÁŽ KAVIAREŇ</td></tr>
<tr><td colspan="2">M R Štefánika 48, Martin; tel: 0905
260 364; €
First-floor café with a range of cakes
and ices and a good view from the
window seats of Martin's strikingly
refurbished town centre. Can get
rather smoky.</td></tr>
<tr><td colspan="2">④ HARLEY-DAVIDSON
CHOPPER CLUB</td></tr>
<tr><td colspan="2">Franc. Partizánov, Vrútky;
tel: 043 428 6880; €€
American-style dining in a Harley-
themed, barn-like establishment on
the main road leading out of Martin
towards the gorge of the River Váh.
Famous for particularly juicy, tender
and tasty steaks.</td></tr>
</table>

paying a parking fee you must also buy
a ticket to enter the village; it is well
worth while, since this is probably the
best place in the country to experience
the atmosphere of a typical Slovak
rural settlement, with brightly painted
log farmhouses facing gable-on to the
steeply rising, unpaved main street.

Unlike the many other open-air collections of folk architecture, Vlkolínec
is still lived in, though some of its
buildings now serve as holiday homes.
One, the **Roľnický dom**, is a museum,
while another houses an information
centre. The most picturesque corner of
this idyllic little place is where a
detached timber bell tower stands
close to a bubbling fountain.

MARTIN

Return to Ružomberok and drive west
through the mountains on road no. 18/
E50 along valley of the Váh. After 29km
(18 miles), leave the main road and
enter the town of **Martin ⑥**. Boosted
under Communism as an industrial
centre, with a huge and now largely
derelict factory producing tanks for the
armies of the Warsaw Pact, Martin
played a key role in the 19th- and early
20th-century development of Slovak
national consciousness, and was even
considered at one point as a possible
capital for the newly emergent nation.

The Museums

It is the home of insitutions such as the
National Library, the National Ceme-
tery, and the **Slovak National Museum**
(Slovenské národné muzeum; Tue–

Sun 9am–5.30pm; charge), with the country's most comprehensive collection of folk arts.

Lovers of painting will be intrigued by the town's **Martin Benku Museum** (Múzeum Martina Benku; Tue–Fri 9am–4pm, Sat 9am–5pm; charge), the residence and studio of the artist Martin Benka (1888–1971), the devoted recorder of the traditional Slovak landscape and its hard-working inhabitants. Others may want to visit the **Museum of the Slovak Village** (Múzeum slovenskej dediny; May–Aug: Tue–Sun 9am–6pm, Sept–Apr: Tue–Fri, Sun 10am–2.30pm; charge), the most extensive of its kind in Slovakia. As well as dwellings and farmhouses brought from various parts of the country, it has many other kinds of traditional buildings, including churches. If it is time for a snack, visit the **Pasáž Kaviareň**, see ⑪③.

With a chairlift (possibly out of action) and a single-track mountain road giving access beyond the tree-line to the meadows of **Martinské hole** (1,476m/4,842ft), Martin makes a good alternative centre for hikes in the Malá Fatra.

END OF THE TOUR

After rejoining road no. 18, drive west towards Žilina. Hungry drivers can stop for a steak at the **Harley-Davidson Chopper Club**, see ⑪④. The busy highway hugs the banks of the Váh as the river pierces the Malá Fatra massif in a deep, meandering ravine, its flanks clad in glorious woodland. The far end of the gorge is guarded by two venerable castles: one, the **Old Castle** (Starý hrad), is in a state of romantic ruin, while the other, **Strečno Castle** ❼ (Hrad Strečno; Tue–Sun, mid-Apr– June: 9am–5pm, July–Aug: 9am–6pm, Sept–Oct: 9am–4pm; charge) is partly restored and offers splendid views over river, forests and mountains, albeit after a steep climb on foot.

Continuing on the main road brings you back to Žilina.

Strečno Castle
It is probably best to leave the climb up to this crag-top stronghold for another time. Access to it when coming from Martin involves a tricky left-hand turn across what is often a constant stream of traffic.

'Father of the Nation'

Ružomberok was the home town of the Catholic priest Andrej Hlinka (1864–1938), a doughty fighter for the rights of the Slovak people, first against their Hungarian rulers, then against the centralising tendencies of the government of Czechoslovakia in far-off Prague. In 1907, local villagers rioted when Hlinka's Hungarian bishop forbade him to attend the consecration of his new church. News of the ensuing massacre by Hungarian gendarmes shocked Europe, and helped prepare the ground for the dissolution of the Austro-Hungarian Empire. Following the creation of the new state of Czechoslovakia in 1918, Hlinka's insistence on autonomy for Slovakia was a constant irritation for the politicians in Prague. His posthumous reputation suffered because of the wartime activities of the 'Hlinka Guard', black-uniformed bully-boys modelled on the German SS. He remains a symbol, albeit a controversial one, of Slovak independence, and is still revered by many today. His portrait graces Slovakia's 1,000-crown banknote.

SILVER AND GOLD

A day exploring the country's heartland, where well-preserved medieval mining towns protected by mighty strongholds are set among wonderfully forested mountains and uplands.

Caves at Harmanec
These limestone caves contain spectacular, snow-white stalactites and stalagmites. However, it is worth noting that there is a long walk from the car park to the cave entrance, so this trip is best left for another day.

Below: National Uprising Museum.

DISTANCE 145km (90 miles) return from Banská Bystrica
TIME A whole day
START/END Banská Bystrica
POINTS TO NOTE

An early start would just about enable you to undertake this tour by train, an unforgettable experience on splendidly engineered lines through the mountains. However, doing the trip by car will reveal just as many scenic delights, as well as avoiding the need to make possibly complicated connections at remote stations. Banská Bystrica is 210km (130 miles) by motorway and mostly dual-carriageway road from Bratislava, and minimum 3½ hours by train.

This tour begins in the bustling regional capital, Banská Bystrica, takes a winding pass road over the Veľká Fatra massif, descends briefly into the fertile Turiec valley, then climbs again before descending into 'golden' Kremnica, home of the country's mint. A further descent and ascent lead to 'silver' Banská Štiavnica, its mining and architectural heritage protected by Unesco designation. The return to Banská Bystrica is via Zvolen, overlooked by its castle, the home of an important art collection.

BANSKÁ BYSTRICA

Rising from the banks of the River Hron, **Banská Bystrica ❶** has a swaggering air, no doubt because of its unrivalled position as the principal urban centre of central Slovakia. Recent nationalist-minded governments have boosted the city in an attempt to make it a counterweight to sophisticated, over-Westernised Bratislava. Like the other old mining towns of the region, Banská Bystrica's history goes far back into the Middle Ages, to the time when Hungarian kings invited experts from Germany to settle here and exploit the rich mineral deposits. Copper and silver were the sources of Banská Bystrica's early prosperity, enabling its leading citizens to build

themselves the fine mansions that line the town's spacious main square.

Exploring the Town

The leaning Renaissance clocktower on the main square offers a great view of the whole city. Higher up still is the town's citadel, a complex of barbican, town hall and churches. In the **Church of Our Lady** (Panna Mária), do not miss the superb medieval altarpiece carved by the incomparable Master Paul of Levoča *(see p.69)*. A masterly piece of Baroque carving, featuring Jesus and his disciples, stands outside just by the main entrance door.

Unlike the other towns on this tour, Banská Bystrica continued to prosper even after the exhaustion of its mineral resources. In 1944, it was from here that the Slovak National Uprising was co-ordinated, and it is here that this stirring chapter in the nation's history is best commemorated. Housed in a striking 1960s building reminiscent of an alien space station, the **SNP Museum** (Múzeum SNP; Tue–Sun, May–Sept: 9am–6pm, Oct–Apr: 9am–4pm; charge) has excellent displays explaining the Uprising and putting it in the context of other European resistance movements during World War II.

Above from far left: Kremnica rooftops; the view towards SNP Square.

Below left: the churches of Our Lady and the Holy Cross, Banská Bystrica.

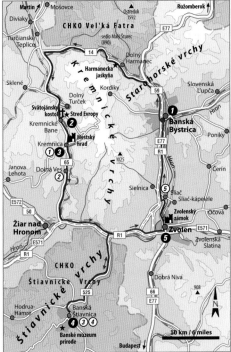

Slovak Semmering

Named after the world-renowned stretch of mountain railway in Austria, the line linking Zvolen with Kremnica climbs nearly 500m (1,640ft) on its way northwards out of the valley of the River Hron. It is one of the most spectacular railway journeys in the country, not least because cost considerations meant that the track winds round the contours of the hills rather than overcoming them by means of tunnels and bridges.

TOWARDS KREMNICA

Head north from Banská Bystrica on main road no. 59/E77, turning left after 8km (5 miles) towards Turčianske Teplice and Martin and at Dolný Harmanec passing the car park that gives access to the Harmanec caves (Harmanecká jaskyňa). The serpentine road climbs over the Malý Šturec pass (890m/2,920ft) through the glorious forests of the Veľká Fatra massif, unlike the railway line which mostly bores its way through the mountains in a series of tunnels. Shortly after emerging from the forest, turn left on road no. 65 towards Žiar nad Hronom. A short detour to the left (signposted

'Stred Evropy') to the village of Kremnické Bane brings you to the isolated, beautifully sited **Church of St John** (Svätojánsky kostol) and a **monument** ❷ marking what is considered (by Slovak geographers at least) to be the very centre of the European continent.

Golden Kremnica

Return to the main road and continue into **Kremnica** ❸. The high-yielding seams of 'Golden' Kremnica may have been exploited as early as the 11th century, but the town's glory days came later, in the 14th century and after, when the Hungarian royal mint was established here. Now the Slovak state mint, it is still in operation, its history well

Slovak National Uprising

The Slovak National Uprising (Slovenské Národné Povstanie or SNP) of August/September 1944 took place at the same time as the far more famous Warsaw Uprising, and, like it, was defeated. It represented an attempt to overthrow the regime led by President Tiso, the nationalist cleric who had collaborated with Hitler to achieve nominal Slovak independence. By this stage in the war, with the Soviet army approaching from the east, it was clear that Germany and her allies faced defeat. To save Slovak honour and enable the country to gain its rightful place in postwar Czechoslovakia, elements of the Slovak army and resistance groups prepared a coup d'état to take control of the country and open the Carpathian passes, enabling the Russians to sweep westwards towards Vienna in a thrust that could conceivably bring the war to a rapid end. Unfortunately, undisciplined partisans jumped the gun by murdering a German military mission as it passed through the town of Martin, and the Uprising had to be unleashed prematurely. Despite having only limited resources at their disposal, the Germans reacted swiftly; they succeeded in occupying most of Slovakia within days, though it took them two months to batter their way into the mountainous redoubt around Banská Bystrica. Despite the defeat of the Uprising, many soldiers and partisans escaped into the forests and mountains and carried out guerrilla operations in the bitter winter of 1944/45, easing the Russian advance the following spring.

documented in the **Museum of Coins and Medals** (Múzeum mincí a medailí; Tue–Sun May–Sept: 9am–1pm, 2–5.30pm, Oct–Apr: 9am–1pm, 2–4.30pm; charge). Kremnica has hardly grown since the Middle Ages, and its steeply sloping main square is little more than a village green, albeit enhanced by stately town mansions and a splendid Baroque plague column. One of the town's best restaurants, the **Silvanus**, see ⑪①, is also situated here.

Kremnica's Castle

It is well worth while climbing up to the **Town Castle** (Mestský hrad; May–Sept: Tue–Sun 8.30am–noon, 1–5.30pm, Oct–Apr: Tue–Sat 8.30am–noon, 1–4.30pm; charge), a restored complex of church, rotunda, defensive towers and double ramparts with a number of small museums. But the main attraction is the view over the town and the rolling uplands.

BANSKÁ ŠTIAVNICA

Continue south on road no. 65. If you did not eat in Kremnica, the **Koliba**, see ⑪②, is the place to stop off. Back on the road, at the intersection with motorway R1/E571 head east in the direction of Zvolen as far as the next interchange, where you leave the motorway and drive south on road no. 525 towards Banská Štiavnica.

Built on hills, and nowadays well off the beaten track, 'silver' **Banská Štiavnica** ❹ has shrunk since it was the third-largest town in the Hungarian kingdom. Nor, despite its Unesco des-

ignation, has it yet attracted the kind of international tourism that its rich historical and architectural heritage merits. Apart from anything else, this means you will almost certainly be able to park in the very heart of town

Trinity Square

The steeply sloping Námestie sv. Trojice (Trinity Square) is named after its most obvious monument, the exceptionally extravagant Baroque Trinity Column *(see p.54)*, erected in the middle of the 18th century to mark deliverance from the plague. The square is lined with town mansions of various dates; one particularly fine example is the **Jozef Kollár Gallery** (Galéria Jozefa Kollára; May–Sept: Wed–Mon 9am–5pm, Tue 9am–7pm, Oct–Apr: Mon–Fri 8am–4pm; charge), worth entering for its lovely

---

Food and Drink ⑪

① SILVANUS
Štefánikovo námestie 33–40, Kremnica; tel: 045 674 4881; €
Right on the main square, dine off carefully prepared game dishes in the historic ambience of one of Kremnica's venerable town mansions. Summer eating in the courtyard, with a fountain to keep you cool and play equipment to distract the children. Service can be a little slow.

② KOLIBA
Dolná Ves; no tel; €
Just over 5km (3 miles) south of Kremnica, on the right of the main road, this modest-looking timber chalet serves excellent and inexpensive Slovak specialities.

Above from far left: coin at the Museum of Coins and Medals, Kremnica; view towards the Old Town, Banská Štiavnica; monument marking the centre of Europe.

Coining it In!
Among the many fascinating exhibits in Kremnica's Museum of Coins and Medals is an ancient coining press. You can observe how money used to be minted or even stamp a commemorative coin of your own.

The Clapper
On the way up to Banská Štiavnica's New Castle, the tower-like Klopačka building housed the clapper, which was sounded to summon the miners to begin their arduous shift. Nowadays the clapper is sounded just for the amusement of tourists, while the building contains a teahouse.

interiors as well as for artworks dating from the 13th to the 20th centuries.

The Old and New Castles

Nearby, a path winds up to the **Old Castle** (Starý zámok; May–Oct: daily 9am–5pm, Nov–Apr: Mon–Fri 8am–4pm; charge), a medieval fortress strengthened in the 16th century as Hungary came increasingly under Turkish domination. But the real attraction of Banská Štiavnica is its ever-changing townscape, a series of delightful pictures composing themselves as you wander up and down its cobbled streets, frequently with views out to the surrounding hills. One

The Turkish Peril
For nearly two centuries, the lowlands of Hungary were occupied by the Ottoman Empire. In their mountain fastness, the Slovaks remained relatively undisturbed, but precautions had to be taken against Turkish raiding parties in search of slaves and booty, hence the construction of fortresses and lookout posts such as Štiavnica's New Castle.

summit is crowned with a Baroque **Kalvária**, a series of stations of the Cross leading up to a pilgrimage chapel visible for miles around. An even more prominent structure is the bright-white **New Castle (**Nový zámok; May–Sept: Wed–Mon 9am–5pm, Tue 9am–7pm, Oct–Apr: Mon–Fri 8am–4pm; charge), new only when it was built in the mid-16th century to give advance warning of the approach of marauding Turks. It now contains displays on this stormy episode in Slovakia's history.

Among the town's restaurants, **Hotel Grand Matej**, see ⑪③, and **Reštaurácia u Böhma**, see ⑪④, are both recommended.

The Open-Air Mining Museum

The most fascinating of the town's several mining-themed museums is on the southwestern outskirts; the **Open-Air Mining Museum (**Banské múzeum v prirode; May–Oct: Mon–Sat 9am–5pm, Sun 9am–7pm, Apr: Tue–Sun 8am–4pm; charge), laid out on the site of a 16th-century mine, offers a number of surface exhibits as well as the chance to descend into the bowels of the earth and experience something of the conditions endured by the medieval workforce.

ZVOLEN

Leave Banská Štiavnica the way you came, and on reaching the motorway follow signs to **Zvolen ❺**. Still surrounded by seemingly endless forests, in the Middle Ages this used to be a

---

Food and Drink 🍴

③ HOTEL GRAND MATEJ
Kammerhofská 5, Banská Štiavnica;
tel: 045 692 1231; €
The best hotel in Štiavnica has a most attractive restaurant and a shaded summer terrace.

④ REŠTAURÁCIA U BÖHMA
Strieborná 7, Banská Štiavnica; tel:
903 525 022; €
A pretty pink-painted building of great antiquity houses a vaulted restaurant serving regional and international dishes.

⑤ HOTEL KASKÁDY
Letecká 12, Sliač; tel: 045 544 1122; €€–€€€
It is worth turning off the motorway between Zvolen and Banská Bystrica just to experience this amazing establishment, a tour de force of luxurious styling in the manner of Donald Trump. Gastronomic restaurant, bar and *koliba* serving Slovak specialities.

favourite resort of Hungarian monarchs escaping from the intense summer heat of Budapest.

Zvolen Castle

Zvolen Castle (Zvolenský zámok; May–Sept: Tue–Sun 10am–5.30pm, Oct–Apr: Wed–Sun 10am–5.45pm; charge) was originally built by one of their number in the 14th century as a hunting lodge. Later it was strengthened in the face of the Ottoman threat to become the formidable stronghold that looms over the town today. Now part of the Slovak National Gallery, it is here rather than in Bratislava that you can see many of the gallery's collection of European Old Master paintings, as well as copies of medieval Master Paul of Levoča's sublime sculptures.

Motorway E77 brings you swiftly back to Banská Bystrica. If you have time, turn off the motorway for a peek (or why not enjoy a drink or even a meal) inside the extravagant **Hotel Kaskády**, see ⑪⑤.

Left: Slovak countryside in winter.

MOUNTAIN LAKES

An undemanding but occasionally rocky walk, this tour links the two largest and most beautiful mountain lakes in the High Tatras, lakes Štrba and Poprad, starting at the Tatras' highest resort and leading to one of their most popular chalet restaurants.

The 'Kalamita'

On the afternoon of 19 November 2004, a terrible wind tore through the High Tatras, reaching speeds of up to 180kph (112mph) and laying waste to 120 sq km (46 sq miles) of forest. Shocked by scenes of utter devastation, many thought the area would never recover. But the worst-affected woodland consisted of monotonous plantations of spruce; the higher-level, more natural forest was largely spared, and the mountains themselves remained inviolate. The tree trunk above shows Kalamita damage.

Right: signposts on the Magistrala trail.

DISTANCE 9km (5½ miles)

TIME Approx. 1hr 30 mins for the outward walk, 1hr 15 mins return

START/END Štrbské Pleso

POINTS TO NOTE

The return can be made along the way you came, or by descending on a surfaced road to Popradské Pleso rail station, from where there are trains roughly every hour to take you to Štrebské Pleso in just a few minutes. Check times before setting out if you intend to return this way. Mountain weather is unpredictable, and it can snow in the Tatras even in summer. Check conditions before setting out and take along rainproof clothing and a sweater. Mountain boots are advisable. The path is closed in winter because of the danger of avalanches. Štrbské Pleso is about 325km (201 miles) from Bratislava. Access by road is off the main Bratislava–Košice route E50. There are two rail connections: by Tatra Electric Railway from the regional centre of Poprad or by cogwheel railway from the village of Tatranská Štrba on the main Bratislava–Košice line.

Part of the long-distance, high-level route known as the 'Tatranská Magistrala', this path leads from one lake, through forest and open terrain, before reaching the other, the site of one of the most visited chalets in the area and an unusual 'symbolic cemetery'.

ŠTRBSKÉ PLESO RESORT

At an elevation of more than 1,300m (4,265ft), the busy resort of **Štrbské**

Pleso 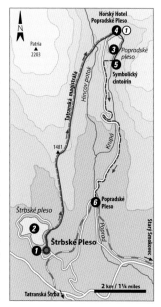 is named after its lovely lake. From here, mountaineers and walkers have direct access to the heights. There are shops, a choice of hotels and the best skiing facilities in Slovakia, including two ski jumps. To the north, valleys gouged out by glaciers lead past waterfalls and highland tarns to a magnificent backdrop of jagged peaks. Among them are Kriváň (2,494m/ 8,182ft), with a distinctive crooked outline that has made it a national symbol and the object of an annual patriotic pilgrimage, and Rysy (2,499m/ 8,199ft), right on the border with Poland and supposedly climbed by none other than Vladimir Ilyich Lenin.

Lake Štrba

From Štrbské Pleso car park or railway station walk the short distance uphill in a northwesterly direction to the **lake** ❷ (also called Štrbské Pleso) itself, in its glorious mountain setting. Here, you join the Magistrala long-distance trail, whose red markings you will follow all the way to your destination.

Turn right along the lakeshore, then right again for a short distance through the forest to join a tarmac road which crosses a bridge. Almost immediately opposite, a footpath leads past an interpretative panel (in Slovak) into the forest. There now begins a steady but not arduous ascent through the spruce trees, which at this height were less affected by the great storm of 2004 *(see left)* than their counterparts at lower levels. The slope eases and you approach a junction with a green-marked path to the right. Continue on the red-marked path, which emerges from the forest to give fine views and then passes through an area of *kosodrevina*, the characteristic blanket of dwarf pines that mark the transition between the upper limit of the forest and bare rock. You now descend to a timber bridge over the **Hincov potok**, a mountain stream that is a tributary of the River Poprad; the bridge and fine upstream views makes this a favourite spot for photographs.

LAKE POPRAD

A short climb from the Hincov brook is followed by a descent to **Lake Poprad** ❸ (Popradské pleso). The 7-hectare (17-acre) lake lies in a wonderful mountain setting, the

Above from far left: the magnificent view from Lake Štrba to the Tatras; hikers checking their route; autumn leaves; Lake Poprad.

It is an Ill Wind… Despite the ravages of the 'Kalamita', visitors continue to come to the High Tatras, and the disaster could turn out to be a blessing in disguise, opening the way to the restoration of a more natural, ecologically robust forest. But controversy continues to rage, with conservationists, logging interests and developers at odds with one another about the future of this vulnerable area.

Reluctant Tourism
The first chalet on the shore of Lake Poprad was built by the mountaineers of the Hungarian Carpathian Club in 1879. Within a year it was a heap of ashes, supposedly burned down by local people fearful of the threat from tourism.

Below: hikers near Lake Poprad.

forest on the lower slopes giving way to soaring crags high above. On its shore rises the **Horský Hotel Popradské Pleso** ❹, the large Lake Poprad chalet, where you are unlikely to be alone; this is one of the most popular destinations in the Tatras for walkers of all abilities, not least because of its location on the Magistrala and because it gives access to a challenging walk into the heart of the mountains parallel to the Hincov torrent. It is also a great place for a fortifying meal, see ⑪①.

SYMBOLIC CEMETERY

The chalet and its superb surroundings are certain to whet your appetite for further exploration of the High Tatras, though you would be well advised to get fully fit before attempting the continuation of the Magistrala, which climbs up eastward via an endless seeming series of zig-zags to a high pass. For the moment, it is probably best to confine yourself to a short extension to today's walk.

Follow the Magistrala until it turns left away from the lake. Continue along the shore to join a yellow-marked path, turning uphill after 400m (1,312ft) to the **Symbolic Cemetery** ❺ (Symbolický cintorín).

Watched over by a tiny white chapel with a shingle roof, the cemetery was laid out in the late 1930s in memory of those losing their lives in the mountains. No-one is actually buried

---

Food and Drink 🍴
① HORSKÝ HOTEL POPRADSKÉ PLESO
Štrbské Pleso; tel: 052 449 2177; €
The Lake Poprad chalet is really a mountain hotel, with dozens of fairly basic rooms enjoying fine views from their dormer windows. The large restaurant buzzes with activity at most times of the day, with hikers downing hearty helpings of sustaining Slovak food. On some guides and maps it is shown with its earlier name of Chata kapitána Morávku (Captain Moravka Chalet), honouring a partisan leader killed in action the last weeks of World War II.

here, but the number of memorials increases yearly as the mountains continue to claim victims.

The Return

Go back along the yellow-marked path to the lake and rejoin the Magistrala in order to descend to Štrbské Pleso the way you came. Alternatively, turn left along the path and left again along the surfaced road that descends gently through the forest to the **Popradské pleso station ⑥**, where you can catch the electrical railway train to Štrbské Pleso (having first purchased a ticket from the machine on the platform). Using the train in this way cuts out what could prove to be a mildly tiring climb at the end of the day, since Popradské pleso station is some 100m (328ft) below the finishing point of the walk.

Tatra Fauna: Bears

Brown bears live in the mountains of much of central and northern Slovakia, including the High Tatras. Their precise number is unknown, though it is probably less than 1,000. Most keep well away from human beings, and you are extremely unlikely to encounter one while walking in the Tatras, least of all on one of the popular routes described in this guide. Overcoming their shyness, some bears have become addicted to goodies that humans provide, descending from the forest to raid village waste bins for scraps of food rather than relying on their natural diet of berries. Such rogue animals are sometimes caught and removed to remote areas by the wildlife and forestry service. It is almost unheard of for bears to attack people. The very few incidents that do occur are usually the result of foolish behaviour on the part of the person concerned. If you do meet a bear, avoid eye contact and move slowly and calmly away. Never come between a mother bear and her cubs. If attacked, a submissive attitude is more likely to pacify the bear than violent resistance.

Early Visitors
In the past, apart from a few shepherds and foresters, local people shunned the mountains, finding them harsh and frightening. The first recorded ascent of a Tatra peak was by David Fröhlich from Kežmarok, in 1615, while in 1793 several summits were conquered by an intrepid Scottish traveller, Robert Townson. Tourism only began to take off in the late 19th century, with the construction of grand hotels and the inauguration of an express train service patronised by rich leisure-seekers from Budapest.

ALONG THE
MAGISTRALA

Mountain railways give easy access to an enjoyable section of the Magistrala long-distance trail. The moderately demanding uphill route goes through forest and scree, past torrents and waterfalls and offers magnificent mountain panoramas.

Novel Descent
The summer equivalent of whizzing down from Hrebienok to Starý Smokovec on skis or by toboggan is to hire a *kolobežka*, a 'mountain scooter' *(shown above, bottom)*, and set off down the road.

DISTANCE 4km (2 miles)
TIME Around 2 hrs for the walk; at least half a day for the whole trip, to enjoy the mountains to the full.
START/END Starý Smokovec
POINTS TO NOTE

The Hrebienok funicular operates 7.30am–7pm. The Skalnaté pleso–Tatranská–Lomnica cable-car operates July–Aug 8.30am–7pm, May–June and Sept–Nov 8.30am–5pm; it can get busy, so it is advisable to book ahead. This section of the Magistrala is well laid out but quite steep in places (total height gain is 466m/1,529ft) and often with a rocky surface; to wear trainers is asking for a twisted ankle, and proper mountain boots are highly recommended. Doing the walk in the uphill direction suggested may be fairly strenuous, but is easier on the joints than going downhill. There is no need to take along a picnic, as meals and refreshments are available at the start and finish of the walk and at the Zamkovského Chalet, but a water-bottle may be advisable on a hot day.

Start in the mountain resort of Starý Smokovec, founded as early as 1793 and accessible by the Tatra Electric Railway. From here a funicular climbs up to Hrebienok, the starting point of the walk. From Skalnaté pleso, where the walk finishes, you descend by cable car to the upper part of the village of Tatranská Lomnica, from where there are trains to Starý Smokovec, Štrbské Pleso (Lake Štrba) and Poprad.

Food and Drink 🍴

① ZAMKOVSKÉHO CHATA
Starý Smokovec; tel: 052 442 2636; €

A typical timber-built mountain hut, the Zamkovského Chata was built in 1943 by a famous Tatra mountaineer and guide, Štefan Zamkovský. In Communist times it was nationalised and given the name of Captain Nálepka, a partisan commander who fell on the Eastern Front. Once more in the ownership of the Zamkovský family, it has a cosy interior with plenty of mementos of exploits among the peaks. You may find your dining companions fortifying themselves with a plateful of *buchty*, jam doughnuts, but unless you have a particularly sweet tooth, a *guláš* lunch might be a better bet.

HREBIENOK

Starting its ascent from just above the Hotel Grand in **Starý Smokovec ❶**, the Hrebienok funicular enables you to avoid the rather tedious climb on foot through the forest above the village, devastated by the 'Kalamita' storm *(see p.56)*. Stand at the lower end of the carriage if you want to enjoy the ever-widening view over the mountain slopes and the valley beyond. The funicular (built 1906–8) takes about seven minutes to reach its upper station at **Hrebienok ❷**, 1,285m (4,216ft) above sea level. With the Hotel Sorea (restaurant and self-service canteen) and the Bílikova chalet, Hrebienok is a popular wintersports area, with ski lifts and a toboggan run down to Starý Smokovec.

TOWARDS THE ZAMKOVSKÉHO CHALET

Look for the signpost just to the east of the Hotel Sorea indicating Skalnaté Pleso, with the Magistrala identified by red markings. The route heads off into the forest, and in about 15 minutes you reach a junction from which a path leads down to the right to the waterfalls of the fast-flowing **Cold Stream ❸** (Studený potok) and the Rainerova chalet. You can pause at the junction to admire the falls, then continue along the main path, which crosses the torrent by means of a timber bridge, then zig-zags uphill to cross an equally impressive tributary of the Studený potok. Stop on the bridge here and look upstream to a spectacular narrow waterfall, before setting off again along the path, which soon leaves the forest and enters the *kosodrevina* zone with its cover of dwarf pines, occasional birches and rowans. This section of the route is particularly stony and consequently unkind to the ill-shod, and you will probably be glad to reach the welcoming **Zamkovského chata ❹**. Set back in the forest, and almost exactly halfway along the route, this chalet is the ideal place to join other hikers for a convivial drink or meal, see 🍴①.

SKALNATÉ PLESO

Once you are ready, set off quite steeply uphill to one of the high points of the walk, the **Lomnica Viewpoint ❺**

Above from far left: hiking the Magistrala; cable-cars from Skalnaté Pleso.

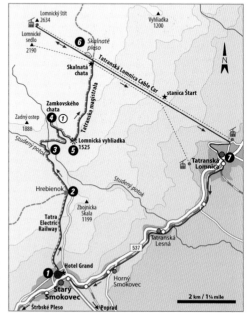

Above from left:
Lomnický štít viewing
platform; rafters on
the River Dunajec.

(Lomnická vyhliadka), which looks out over a vast panorama of mountain, forest and plain with the town of Poprad visible in the distance. You now climb steadily through the *kosodrevina,* over scree and avalanche channels, eventually passing in front of the Skalnatá chalet, then zigzagging up to the top station of the Tatranská Lomnica cable car.

Lake Views

You could descend straightaway, but it makes sense to pause for a while to take in the spectacular surroundings of **Skalnaté pleso ❻** (the name means 'rocky lake'), 1,751m (5,745ft) above sea level. The mountain lake lies in a superb basin defined by ridges running down from one of the giants of the Tatras, Lomnický štít. At 2,634m (8,642ft) the mountain is second only to Gerlachovský štít, 7km (4 miles) to the southwest and the highest peak in the whole of the Carpathians.

Cable-Car Rides

If there is space (to be sure of a place, book a day or two in advance; ask at your hotel for details), you could board the cable-car and swing over the abyss to the summit of Lomnický štít, where the mountain-top has been tamed with handrails and even a café. Another possibility is to take a trip up to a lower ridge, Lomnické sedlo, by chairlift. Otherwise buy your ticket for the descent to Tatranská Lomnica and climb aboard one of the modern gondolas which have replaced the old cable-car. Do not make the mistake of alighting at the first station you come to; called Štart, this is only halfway down to your destination.

Tatranská Lomnica

At the cable-car terminus there is a cluster of souvenir stalls around a car park and a useful information centre, which sometimes shows old films of the construction of the cable railway in the 1940s. Go down the road from the car park to a T-junction and straight across to a footpath which leads to **Tatranská Lomnica railway station**. From here there are trains roughly once an hour back to Starý Smokovec (and Štrbské Pleso).

Tatra Fauna

While an encounter with a bear is only a remote possibility during your walks in the mountains, there is a good chance of coming across both marmots and chamois, particularly in open rocky areas. Members of the squirrel family, marmots live in groups in burrows. On the surface, they sit bolt upright to look out for intruders, signalling the approach of danger with a sharp whistle. The symbol of the Tatras, the agile chamois can often be glimpsed high up on cliffs and steep slopes in what seem to be impossibly precarious positions.

RAFTING ON THE RIVER DUNAJEC

This classic excursion takes you by road from the High Tatras to the tiny Pieniny national park, a massif of intensely folded limestone pierced by the dramatic gorge of the River Dunajec. The course of the winding river can be followed on foot, by bike, but best of all aboard a raft.

From Starý Smokovec, head east along the Cesta Slobody/Freedom Road through the High Tatra resorts, turning right 8km (5 miles) beyond Tatranská Lomnica on road no. 67 towards Kežmarok. Turn left on to road no. 542 as you enter Spišská Bela in the direction of Červený Kláštor. The road climbs steeply up the flanks of the Spišská Magura mountains to the **Magurské sedlo** (pass) ❶. To the north is the gloriously undulating countryside of the **Zamagurie** region, literally 'beyond the Magura', an area whose ownership has frequently been disputed between the rulers of Poland and Slovakia. It is one of the homelands of the Goral people.

DOWN THE DUNAJEC

Just beyond the straggling small town of Spišská Stará Ves, turn right on to road no. 543 towards the village of Červený Kláštor. The road runs parallel to the River Dunajec, which here forms the frontier between Slovakia and Poland. Beyond the village of Majere but before you arrive in Červený Kláštor itself, you will see one of several **rafting stations** ❷ on the Slovak bank of the river. The rafts consist of several pontoon-like

DISTANCE Around 125km (77 miles) return trip

TIME A full day

START Starý Smokovec

END Červený Kláštor

POINTS TO NOTE

The drive to and from the Dunajec takes a good hour each way, the rafting trip about 90 mins. Allow time for the return on foot, bike or other means of transport to Červený Kláštor. Coach excursions run from the Tatra resorts; most include a Goral-style meal after the rafting trip. With your own car you will be free to stop wherever you fancy in what is a highly scenic area and perhaps prolong your stay in Červený Kláštor. The route can be undertaken from any of the resorts in the High Tatras.

structures lashed together, taken apart at the end of each trip and returned to the starting point by lorry. They are quite safe, though their plank seating is not kind to anyone with back trouble. Unless you have booked ahead as a group *(see margin, p.64)* you may have to wait until a sufficient number of passen-

Gorals

The ethnographic group known as the Gorals lives in a number of areas in the Polish-Slovak borderlands. No one is quite sure where their distant ancestors came from, though it may have been from the Balkans. Their near-impenetrable dialect (for Slovaks) is based on Polish, with the addition of many Slovak words. Just as Arabic has any number of terms for 'camel', and Inuit a similar array for different kinds of snow, Goral has a rich vocabulary for sheep-rearing, and has even given Slovak the word *bryndza* (sheep cheese), used in that unavoidable national dish, *bryndzové halušky* *(see p.15)*.

Above from left:
view of Trzy Koruny;
raftsmen sport
traditional costumes;
Goral wooden house
in Červený Kláštor.

Rafting Bookings
Places aboard a raft,
along with arrange-
ments for your return
(bike, minibus, etc) can
be booked at various
points, including the
station mentioned in
the text: Združenie
Pltnikov Dunajec s.r.o
Majere 34 061 01
Spišská Stará Ves;
tel: 052 482 2840;
www.pltnictvo.sk.

gers have assembled. This is unlikely to take long, as this is one of the most popular excursions in the whole of Slovakia.

Once aboard, admire the skill of your raftsman as he propels his craft downstream, soon passing beneath the elegant footbridge linking the village of Červený Kláštor to the Polish bank.

On the Boat

The gorge and national park are entered just beyond the village. By Slovak standards, the Pieniny mountains are not particularly high. The triple peak you see directly ahead of you, **Trzy Koruny/ Three Crowns** , reaches just 982m (3,222ft), but it is the limestone cliffs dropping sheer to the river that make the trip such a spectacular experience, clad as they are with pristine forest of

beech, fir and an extraordinarily rich ground flora. Eagles, storks and lynx live here, while the river itself is home to otters and their favourite prey, trout.

In a straight line, it is only 3km (2 miles) from Červený Kláštor to the point where you disembark, but the river's meanderings mean that the trip covers over 8km (5 miles). The bends are so confusing that it is often impossible to tell whether what you are looking at ahead is in Slovakia or Poland. Your raftsman will almost certainly challenge you to guess which, as well as entertaining you with a variety of anecdotes. At various points he will guide you over rapids, none of which should upset even the most timid of travellers. The trip comes to an end at a point where a side valley, the Lesnica ravine, joins the main

Food and Drink 🍴

① CHATA PIENINY
Lesnica; tel: 052 428 5031; €
This place close to the terminus of the rafting excursion handles large numbers of visitors efficiently. However, far from being a tourist trap, it provides local comestibles in abundance in a cheerfully folksy setting in the chalet itself or outside in a barbecue area.

② GORALSKÁ REŠTAURÁCIA
Červený Kláštor 51; tel: 052 482 2784; www.pltnici.sk; €
The offerings in the souvenir shop may not be to everyone's taste, but the cosy restaurant on the riverside in Červený Kláštor provides reliable Goral-themed food and drink. This is one of several places in and around the village where raft trips and other excursions can be arranged.

③ DUNAJEC VILLAGE
Červený Kláštor 12; tel: 052 482 2027; €
With its various buildings scattered among the trees about 1km (just over ½ mile) on the road leading southeast out of Červený Kláštor, Dunajec Village provides a variety of accommodation as well as standard dishes served in a pleasantly airy dining room free from the folksy ornamentation prevalent elsewhere.

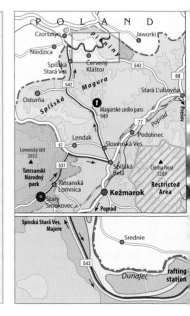

gorge, and close to where the Polish frontier crosses the river.

The riverside pathway continues into Poland, but you will not be able to cross the border here unless you have a Slovak or Polish identity card. A five-minute walk from the disembarkation point brings you to a large chalet, the **Chata Pieniny ❹**, with an extensive open area where all kinds of 'Goral' refreshments are available, see 🍴①.

ČERVENÝ KLÁŠTOR

From the Chata Pieniny you can return to your boarding point by service bus, minibus or taxi (a scenic 16-km/10-mile trip over a pass in the mountains), or by hired bike or on foot along the riverside path, an ancient trade route. In the village of **Červený Kláštor ❺** you could take the time to visit the **Carthusian monastery** (Kartuziánský kláštor; Apr–Oct: daily 9am–5pm; charge) that gives the village its name (Červený Kláštor means 'Red Monastery', so called because of the reddish stone originally used in the monastery's construction).

Founded in the early 14th century by the Carthusians, the monastery still has its Gothic church, though most of its buildings were Baroquised in the 18th century. It is now home to a variety of displays, including photographs of local life in the recent past and a number of magnificent Baroque church sculptures.

A good meal can be had at **Goralská Reštauraciá**, see 🍴②, or slightly further away, at **Dunajec Village**, see 🍴③. Return to the Tatras the way you came.

Clever Cyprian

In its time, the monastery at Červený Kláštor was an important centre of learning, its most illustrious inmate in the 18th century being one Brother Cyprian, doctor, inventor and herbalist, the 'master of 1,000 crafts'. But the flying machine in which he is supposed to have soared from the top of Trzy Koruny to the Tatras is not on show.

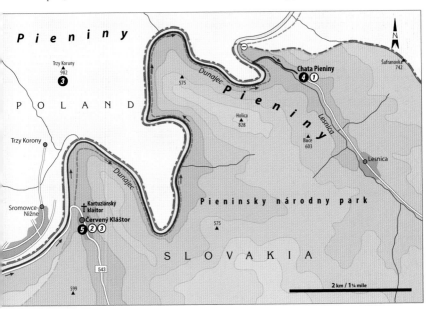

10

SPIŠ COUNTRY

A day's drive taking in the principal sights of this distinctive region at the foot of the Tatras, including two ancient, German-founded towns, the mightiest castle in Central Europe and the unique ecclesiastical settlement of Spišská Kapitula.

Cheese Centre

Kežmarok's German name was Käsmark, meaning 'cheese market'. But as well as a trading centre, it was also a place of learning, with significant educational institutions, including the region's most important German college.

Below: St George's, Spišská Sobota.

DISTANCE Approx. 145km (90 miles) return

TIME A full day

START/END Starý Smokovec

POINTS TO NOTE

Organised excursions by coach take in some of the attractions along this route, but use of a car will give you the time and freedom to savour the special character of the area to the full. We suggest starting and finishing at Starý Smokovec, but this route can be done from any of the High Tatra resorts.

Start the day in the same way as for the excursion to the River Dunajec *(see p.63)* by driving east from Starý Smokovec, though on this occasion only as far as Tatranská Lomnica. Here you turn right towards Poprad and leave the mountains for sweeping, open fields. In the village of Veľká Lomnica, turn right on main road no. 67.

SPIŠSKÁ SOBOTA

Just beyond the industrial village of Matejovce and the motorway, bear right along an (unsignposted) turn into **Spišská Sobota ❶**. Now part of the

Food and Drink

① CUKRÁREŇ FONTANA
Hlavné námestie 50, Kežmarok;
tel: 052 452 4461; €
With a vaulted interior and of course a fountain, this is probably the most pleasant place in Kežmarok in which to enjoy your morning coffee. Very tempting, old-fashioned patisserie too.

② REŠTAURÁCIA HOTEL CLUB
MUDr Alexandra 24, Kežmarok;
tel: 052 452 4051; €
Hunting trophies galore decorate the fresh, modernised interior of this establishment, an indication of the tasty game specialities which form the mainstay of the menu.

much larger town of Poprad, this little jewel of a place consists of a single, funnel-shaped street running along a ridge parallel to the River Poprad. The street is lined with the beautifully restored houses of the burghers and craftsmen who made Spišská Sobota one of the principal towns of the Spiš district in medieval times and later.

St George's Church

In the centre, a stately group of buildings consists of the Town Hall, a bell tower and **St George's Church** (sv. Juraj; May–Oct: Mon–Sat 9am–5pm, or key from parish house opposite; charge payable at bell tower). The church's great treasure is its collection of altarpieces, above all the wonderful St George's altar; the work of Master Paul of Levoča *(see p.69)* and his pupils, it shows the saint in the act of dispatching his fearsome opponent while the threatened maiden prays in the background. Beneath, the half-humorous depiction of the Last Supper has the disciples seemingly oblivious to the words of Jesus.

KEŽMAROK

Return to the main road and go back the way you came to **Kežmarok ❷**, one of the principal centres of the Spiš district and with a few good places to eat, such as **Cukráreň Fontana**, see ⑪①, and **Reštaurácia Hotel Club**, see ⑪②.

The town was laid out in the 13th century on an unusual triangular plan, and its streets are still lined with many a late medieval or Renaissance dwelling with the pointed timber gable typical of the area.

Church of the Holy Cross

In the centre of the triangle is a quiet precinct dominated by the **Church of the Holy Cross** (sv. Kríž; June–Sept: Mon–Fri 9am–5pm), next to which rises a white, free-standing bell tower. Adorned with sgraffito-work and fanciful mock-battlements, it is one of several in the Spiš district, emblems of the area's prosperity in the 15th and 16th centuries, when trade and handicrafts flourished. The church itself boasts beautiful vaults and a fine array of statuary and other artworks. Než-

Above from far left: the only street in Spišská Sobota; colourful Kežmarok, one of the main centres in the Spiš district.

The 'Zipper'
This was what the Germans of the Spiš district called themselves. Their ancestors helped repopulate the area following its devastation by the 13th-century Mongol invasion. Like 95 per cent of Slovakia's German inhabitants, they were expelled after World War II.

Royal Rebel
Born in Kežmarok, then part of Hungary, Imre Thököly was the most ambitious of all the great aristocrats who rebelled against Habsburg rule. His aim, pursued in alliance with France and the Ottoman Empire, was nothing less than the crown of Hungary. His rebellion may have ended in failure and exile to Turkey, but patriotic Hungarians still think of him as a national hero, and many cross the border into Slovakia on a pilgrimage to his elaborate tomb.

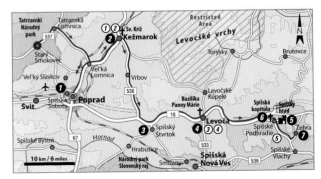

Tolerated Temples
After decades of repression, Protestants were allowed to build themselves a limited number of churches, but only under strict conditions: the buildings had to be constructed of wood without any use of metal (including nails), have no tower or solid foundations, and be sited outside the town walls. Kežmarok's timber church is an outstanding example.

marok's other two great monuments stand at the northern and southern extremities of the town.

The Castle

To the north is the **Castle** (Hrad; May–Sept: Tue–Sun 9am–noon, 1–5pm, Oct–Apr: Mon–Fri guided tour 9am, 10am, 11am, 1pm, 2pm, 3pm; charge), built less to ward off foreign enemies than to keep watch on the independently minded townsfolk (who eventually, in the late 18th century, succeeded in buying it). Medieval in origin, the castle was strengthened and beautified many times; its imposing walls and bastions now shelter an array of museums of local interest.

Timber Church

To the south, just beyond remnants of the town walls, stands a unique group of buildings, among them the **Timber Church** (Drevený kostol; May–Oct: daily 9am–noon, 2–5pm; Nov–Apr: Tue, Fri 10am–noon, 2–4pm; charge). Able to accommodate a congregation of 1,500, this extraordinary structure was erected in the late 17th century. The sober exterior conceals an interior richly decorated in a rather rustic Baroque style, with wall and ceiling paintings and barley-sugar columns.

Other Highlights

Its neighbours include the Lyceum, once a famous place of learning, and an exuberant late 19th-century church in a fusion of styles; it contains the tomb of one of Hungary's great heroes, the magnate Imre Thököly, who led an unsuccessful revolt against the Habsburgs during the late 17th century. His body was only brought here in 1906, long after he had died in Turkish exile.

SPIŠSKÝ ŠVRTOK

Leave Kežmarok on the minor road south that passes through the village of Vrbov before joining main road no. 18/E50, where you turn left toward Levoča. After 2km (just over 1 mile), you cannot fail to notice a church prominently posed on a hilltop site to the right of the road. This is the 13th-century parish church of **Spišský Štvrtok** ❸, made even more of a landmark by its tall tower capped by a spire, sentry-walk and spiky corner pinnacles. Linked to the church is the burial chapel of the powerful princely family of the Zápolyas, an exquisite little Gothic structure modelled on the Sainte-Chapelle in Paris.

Food and Drink 🍴

③ U TROCH APOŠTOLOV
Námestie Majstra Pavla 11, Levoča;
tel: 053 451 4352; €–€€
While the dishes offered are perfectly adequate rather than exceptional, a meal in the 'Three Apostles' offers the chance of dining in the setting of one of Levoča's fine town mansions overlooking the main square. Sumptuous décor and exemplary service.

④ HOTEL U LEVA
Námestie Majstra Pavla 24, Levoča;
tel: 053 450 2311; €–€€
With its own entrance on the main square, this recommended hotel restaurant specialises in refined food with a contemporary touch.

LEVOČA

A further 10km (6 miles), and on the far side of a broad valley the principal destination of this trip, the town of **Levoča** ❹, comes into view, though this first impression gives barely a hint of the riches to come. At this point, continue on the main road along the well-preserved section of ramparts, turning left through the chisel-roofed **Košice Gate** (Košická brána), and parking in **námestie Majstra Pavla**, the spacious square bearing the name of the town's most famous citizen, the great medieval sculptor Master Paul. On the square you will also find **U troch Apoštolov**, see ⑪③, and **Hotel U Leva**, see ⑪④.

Prosperity and Isolation

Situated in a key position on excellent trading routes, Levoča enjoyed centuries of prosperity and power, for a while acting as the capital of the Spiš region. However, a great fire in 1550 was a portent of decline, and the town subsequently became increasingly conservative in its outlook. When the east–west railway was planned through Slovakia in the late 19th century, the citizens of Levoča refused to have anything to do with it; its subsequent isolation has left this late medieval jewel in a near-perfect state of preservation, though its post-Communist restoration remains a work in progress.

Church of St James

Lined with some splendid examples of typical Renaissance town houses, park-like main square forms

a fine setting for the town's principal monuments, foremost among them the **Church of St James (**Sv. Jakub; tours at varying hours; charge). After Košice's cathedral *(see p.84)*, this is the largest Gothic structure in the whole of Slovakia, but it is less the building than its contents that draws visitors from all over the world. The church houses a wealth of carvings by Master Paul and his followers, its centrepiece the stunning high altar, easily the largest of its kind, its finials reaching

Master Paul

Very little is known of the great sculptor we know as Master Paul of Levoča (Majstr Pavol z Levoče in Slovak, Meister Paul von Leutschau in German, 1455–c.1540), not even his surname. He may have been born in Krakow in Poland, where it is possible he learnt his skills in the studio of the far more famous Veit Stoss. By 1500 he had settled in Levoča, where he married, became a town councillor, and ran the workshop which influenced the art of woodcarving over the whole of Slovakia and beyond. His work frequently shows a deep understanding of common humanity, nowhere better expressed than in his depictions of the disciples beneath the high altar in the Church of St James.

The White Lady of Levoča

The walls of Levoča are supposedly haunted by the sad-looking figure of a lady dressed in white. She is the ghost of Julia Korponay, wife of the town commander at the time of the siege of Levoča in the early 18th century. Julia brought disgrace upon herself by clandestinely opening the gates to the enemy, subsequently becoming the mistress of their commander. A dramatic re-enactment of her betrayal, centred on the Town Hall, takes place every summer.

a staggering 18.6m (61ft) into the building's vaults. Beneath Master Paul's more-than-life-size figures of a serene Virgin and Child flanked by St James and St John is his depiction of the Last Supper, in which only an uneasy Judas appears aware of the seriousness of the situation. Further altarpieces and carvings scattered around the interior of the church demonstrate the virtuosity of the master and his followers.

Bear in mind that the primary function of the church is as Levoča's main place of worship; its custodians keep strictly to the official opening hours and do not take kindly to anyone treating it with less than appropriate reverence.

Town Hall

To the south of St James stands the elegant former **Town Hall** (Radnica; daily,

Right: medieval wall-painting in Levoča's Town Hall.

May–Oct: 9am–5pm, Nov–Apr: 8am–4pm; charge), its lovely Renaissance arcades partly cladding an earlier Gothic structure. Trumpeters blast out a proud fanfare from the upper storey at midday every Friday, while the splendid interiors with vaulted or timber-beamed ceilings house the local museum. Its prize exhibit is a famous portrait of Levoča's 'White Lady' *(see left)*.

By the southeast corner of the building is a pillory, a wrought-iron structure called the '**Cage of Shame**', in which female wrongdoers were exposed to the scorn of the public.

Other Sights on the Square

The domed edifice beyond the town hall is the Evangelical Church, built in the early 19th century in a sober, neo-classical style. It is well worth while strolling round the square; most of the mansions lining it have some claim to your attention, none more so than the **Thurzo House** (no. 7) on the east side of the square. Consisting of a pair of Gothic buildings joined together in Renaissance times, it features exuberant gables and sgraffito decoration, the latter added in the 19th century.

At no. 27, a more modest edifice, the **House of Master Paul** (Dom Majstra Pavla; Tue–Sun 9am–5pm; charge) has examples of the great woodcarver's work; though nearly all are copies, they at least give you the chance to see them at close quarters.

Place of Pilgrimage

As you wander around Levoča catch the occasional glimps

to the north of the town. Crowning the summit is a chapel dedicated to the Virgin Mary, the scene every July of Slovakia's greatest Roman Catholic pilgrimage, drawing tens of thousands of enthusiastic worshippers. In 1996 the pilgrims included the Polish Pope John Paul II, who had been here twice before, once as a young chaplain, once as Archbishop of Krákow.

SPIŠ CASTLE

Leave Levoča the way you came in through the Košice Gate and drive east along the main road. As the road begins a long descent after about 10km (6 miles), there appears one of the classic sights of Slovakia, the gaunt ruins of **Spiš Castle** ❺ (Spišský hrad; May–Oct: 9am–7pm, Nov–Apr: by request tel: 053 451 2824; charge) dominating the countryside all around from the limestone crag along which it sprawls. To reach the castle, continue on the main road just past the hill on which it stands and turn sharp right on a minor road, then right again up a track leading to a car park.

The main reward of the uphill walk into the castle is the stupendous view over the Spiš country, the ruins themselves being less impressive close up than when seen from a distance.

Background History
Claimed to be the largest stronghold in Central Europe, the castle was begun by the kings of Hungary in the early 13th century on the site of an older fortress and subsequently vastly extended by the lords of Spiš, notably

Above from far left: architectural detail topping the Town Hall, with the Church of the Holy Cross just visible behind; the magnificently elevated Spiš Castle dominates the landscape.

Left: Levoča's 16th-century 'Cage of Shame', used as a form of punishment.

Above from left:
Spišská kapitula;
hiking in the
'Slovak Paradise'.

by the laying out of a vast lower bailey. It held out against the 13th-century Mongol invasion, but after being ravaged by fire in the late 18th century it gradually fell into decrepitude.

SPIŠSKÁ KAPITULA

Below: the towers of
St Martin's Cathedral,
Spišská kapitula.

From the castle car park return the way you came, turning left on to the main road and left again into the town of Spišské Podhradie. Now continue up the hill and, at the top, turn into the entrance of **Spišská kapitula** ❻. The ecclesiastical counterpart to Spiš Castle, it was from this extraordinary little one-street township that medieval church rulers held sway over the whole region, and it is still the seat of a bishop and a seminary.

St Martin's Cathedral

Its great landmark is the twin-towered **St Martin's Cathedral** (Katedrála sv. Martina; guided tours Mon–Sat 9am, 10am, 11am, 1pm, 2pm, 3pm, 4pm, 4.30pm, Sun 11am, 1pm, 2pm, 3pm, 4pm, 4.30pm; charge, payable at bell tower opposite), founded in the 11th century and extensively restored in the 19th. Inside are fine furnishings including several medieval altarpieces.

Opposite the cathedral is the bishop's palace; to the rear is the seminary, which served as a police college during the Communist era. Lined with the houses of minor church officials, the normally deserted street descends towards a lower gateway and offers an unusual framed view of Spiš Castle in the middle distance.

Chapel Hill
To the west of Spišská Kapitula, a gentle grassy slope leads across the open hilltop to a scatter of buildings including a pilgrimage chapel *(above)*. It is worth the walk for the wonderful view back to the twin-towered cathedral, seen from here against the background of Spiš Castle. The hill is famous as the site of mineral springs, and even of a little geyser.

ŽEHRA

Together, Spiš Castle, Spišská Kapitula and the somewhat run-down town of **Spišské Podhradie** make up an extraordinary grouping of historic buildings and landscape, fully deserving of its Unesco World Heritage status. If you have time, you should visit the fourth and final element in this ensemble, the village church at **Žehra** ❼, 4km (2½ miles) south of Spiš Castle. Unmissable thanks to its elevated position and its onion dome, the little church (key from presbytery if closed) has a unique interior covered in colourful medieval wall-paintings, whose uncovering and restoration involved the use of copious quantities of cottage cheese.

RETURN JOURNEY

Return to the Tatras (and Starý Smoko-vec, our finishing point) via main road no. 18, turning on to road no. 534 as it bypasses Poprad. Before heading home you might like to fortify yourself at the **Spišský Saláš**, see ⑪⑤.

Food and Drink

⑤ SPIŠSKÝ SALÁŠ
Levočská 11, Spišské Podhradie;
tel: 053 454 1202; €
On the road leading back towards Levoča from Spišské Podhradie, this is a highway service area masquerading as a shepherd's hut and providing all the rustic staples of Slovak cuisine. Very tourist-orientated, but none the worse for that, with lots of outdoor facilities and a programme of folksy events. Fine views of Spiš Castle.

SLOVAK PARADISE

Two of the most fascinating features of the Slovak Paradise national park are explored in the course of this round trip from the High Tatras: after a morning's walk in the Hornad river gorge, you drive across the mountains and explore the strange underground world of the Dobšina ice cave.

This tour is easiest taken by car, beginning and ending at any of the High Tatras resorts, such as Starý Smokovec. The two main destinations, Čingov (the gateway to the Slovak Paradise national park) and the Dobšina ice cave, can both be reached by public transport, but you will then more than a day for the trip.

Čingov is accessible by bus from the town of Spišská Nová Ves, 8km (5 miles) to the east and on the main Bratislava–Košice railway line. The Dobšina ice cave is accessible by bus from Spišská Nová Ves and Poprad, and also has its own railway station on the very scenic but ultra-slow single-track line from Banská Bystrica to Košice.

SLOVAK PARADISE NATIONAL PARK

Part of the mountain range running parallel to the Slovak-Hungarian border to the south, and a national park since 1988, the **Slovak Paradise** (Slovenský raj) is a limestone massif with several summits reaching over 1,000m (3,280ft). However, it is not so much the heights that have earned it its name, but the deep and narrow

DISTANCE Around 130km (81 miles) for the drive and 6.5km (4 miles) for the walk
TIME A full day
START/END Starý Smokovec
POINTS TO NOTE
From Starý Smokovec it is 35km (22 miles) to the starting point of the walk, which, with stops for viewing and picnicking, will easily occupy the rest of the morning. The 52-km (32-mile) drive to the Dobšina cave, most of which is on winding and often narrow and poorly surfaced mountain roads, will take well over an hour. From the car park it is a 20-minute uphill walk to the cave entrance, while the tour itself lasts an hour. From here, the 40-km (25-mile) return journey to Smokovec via Poprad is on main roads.

The walk is one of the least demanding in the Slovak Paradise, but stout footwear is highly desirable. The most strenuous section is the 139m (456ft) climb from the river to the lip of the ravine. The average temperature in the Dobšina ice cave is 0°C (32°F), so warm clothing is essential.

Above: gorgeous scenery, harebells and autumn leaves, photographed in 'Slovak Paradise'.

Above from left:
sign for 'Slovak
Paradise'; walkers
looking down from
the Tomášov view-
point; special way-
markers make
navigation easier
and keep walkers
to designated paths.

Below right: the
Tomášov viewpoint
and extraordinarily
sharp drop below.

gorges carved into the limestone by
streams and rivers. Made accessible by
bridges, ladders, chains and catwalks,
these cliff-girt ravines really are a paradise for walkers, who frequent the park
at all times of the year. Flora and fauna
are exceptionally rich, and are subject
to strict protection; much of the area,
with its deep forests of spruce, fir, pine
and larch, is off-limits, and walkers are
required not to stray from the designated, well-marked paths.

HORNAD RAVINE

From the High Tatras, take road no.
534 towards Poprad where you join
road no. 18 and head east towards
Košice. Then, 12km (7 miles) beyond
Poprad, bear right towards Spišská
Nová Ves on road no. 536, turning
right again after 7km (4 miles) towards
Čingov ❶ as you enter the Spišská
Nová Ves suburb of Smižany. Follow
signs to Čingov and park if possible
in the lower car park near the **River
Hornad**, otherwise go back the way
you have come to the overflow car park
higher up.

Places to pause for a drink or a bite
to eat in Čingov include **Penzión Reštaurácia Lesnica**, see ❶①, and the
Hotel Flora, see ❶②; alternatively,
good restaurants in the nearby town of
Spišská Nová Ves include **Nostalgie**,
see ❶③.

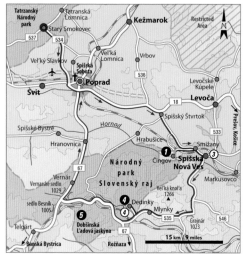

The Walk and Its Highlights

Your main objective on this two-hour walk along the ravine gouged out by the River Hornad is the Tomášov viewpoint (Tomášovský výhľad; *see p.76*). This spectacular rock balcony cantilevered out high above the river is one of the most photographed spots in Slovakia, and features in many a brochure promoting the country's attractions. Most visitors hurry to it as quickly as possible by taking the yellow-marked route from the car park, but it is much more rewarding to follow the blue-marked route along the bottom of the ravine in the direction of Lesnica.

Up to the Viewpoint

Entering the gorge, the blue track runs parallel to the Hornad for a short distance, before turning left at a signboard welcoming you to the national park and crossing the river on a bridge. At the Lesnica-ústie signboard just beyond, a green-marked path takes off to the left, while you continue following the blue marks towards Biely potok-ústie, a precise '31' minutes further on, according to the sign.

Just before you reach this point, the trees open out, and a pretty **meadow** ❷ leads down towards the river. A glance up from here will reveal tiny figures peering down at you from the viewpoint, 139m (456ft) above.

The path now swings round left to the Biely potok-ústie signpost, where you turn right over a little tributary of the Hornad and scramble a short distance up a rocky outcrop. This is the only point on this walk where the park authorities have provided a handhold in the form of chains, but although the rock has been worn smooth by the passage of many feet, this aid is hardly necessary. At the top of the climb, at the Biely potok-rázcestie signpost, the blue route turns west, and it is now time to follow the green-marked path in the direction of the Tomášov viewpoint. This leads you down to a bridge over the Hornad, an attractive spot to linger for a moment.

A short climb away from the river brings you to the 'Pod Tomášovským výhľadom' sign, where you turn right and begin a 25-minute trudge up a zigzag path to the lip of the ravine. At the top of the climb there is no signpost to help you, but look right for green-and-

Waymarks

Throughout Slovakia, hiking trails have been provided with waymarks, which make it virtually impossible to get lost. Red, blue, green and yellow bands between two white stripes appear on trees and other points and on signposts positioned at path junctions. These signposts are often quite elaborate structures; they are named, and give details of altitude and of timed distances to footpath destinations.

Food and Drink 🍴

Your best plan is to carry a picnic and consume it while enjoying the prospect from the Tomášovský výhľad. You will certainly appreciate a refreshing drink after the climb up from the bottom of the ravine.
Places to eat in Čingov include:

① PENZIÓN REŠTAURÁCIA LESNICA
Čingov 113; tel: 053 449 1518; €
Cosy chalet-type establishment conveniently located by the upper car park in Čingov.

② HOTEL FLORA
Čingov; tel: 053 449 1131; €
Dating from Communist times, but partly refurbished, the Flora is probably the best of several hotels scattered around Čingov, and its U Apolónia (Apollo) restaurant has pretensions to style as well as food.

Dobšina Directions
Do not confuse
directions to
Dobšinská L'adová
Jaskyňa/Dobšina Ice
Cave with signs to
Dobšina. The latter
is an old mining
town, a good
16km (10 miles)
from the cave,
and in no sense
a tourist attraction.

yellow marks among the trees and climb through the little cleft in a rock outcrop. To the right, the direct path along the edge of the ravine has been closed because of erosion, so you bear left through a cleared area before emerging on to the **Tomášov view-point ❸** (Tomášovský výhľad).

You are unfortunately unlikely to be alone in savouring the spectacular panorama, which extends over the ravine to the glorious forested hills beyond, and, in clear weather, to the peaks of the High Tatras. Keep away from the sheer drop if you are at all nervous about heights.

The Descent

The entire 50-minute descent to Čingov is along the yellow-marked path. After running parallel to the clifftop, it drops to some chalets and other buildings, where you turn right along a road, then right again at the 'Čingov Džurkovec' signpost by the Autocamping Tatran building. Cross the field, descend through woods, and among some more upmarket chalets bear right and go

Right: hiker on the Hornad river gorge hiking trail.

down a short sharp descent to your starting point.

ACROSS THE MOUNTAINS

From Čingov, drive east to the town of **Spišská Nová Ves** (for a restaurant recommendation, see ⑪③), turning right in the direction of Rožnava as you approach the centre. The road climbs up through the forested uplands of the Slovak Paradise in a series of serpentine bends to the **Grajnár summit** at 1,023m (3,356ft). A 3-km (just over 2-mile) descent brings you to a junction where you bear right towards the village of **Mlynky** along a narrow and badly maintained road.

Around 3.5km (2 miles) beyond Mlynky, a short diversion to the right leads to **Dedinky** ❹. Attractively laid out on the shore of an extensive reservoir, and with the mountains as a backdrop, this large settlement is the main southern gateway to the national park and also has a good place to eat, the **Hotel Priehrada**, see ⑪④.

DOBŠINA ICE CAVE

The main road continues, joining road no. 67, where you should bear right . Some 9km (5 miles) further on you arrive at your destination for the next section of the tour: the **Dobšina Ice Cave** ❺ (Dobšinská Ľadová jaskyňa; 40-minute guided tour June–Aug: 9am, 10am, 11am, noon, 1pm, 2pm, 3pm, 4pm, mid-late May and Sept: 9.30am, 11am, 12.30pm, 2pm; charge). Leave your vehicle in the scruffy car park and make the steep, 20-minute walk up to the cave entrance.

Into the Cave

The ice cave is a near-unique phenomenon, a kind of underground glacier containing more than 110,000 cubic m (144,000 cubic yds) of ice, some of it moulded into strange shapes.

Discovered in 1870, the cave was soon illuminated by electricity and became a tourist attraction, a venue for underground skating competitions. You explore its icy depths by means of slippery steps and catwalks.

To return to the High Tatras, drive west on road no. 67, which turns right in 5km (3 miles) to cross the mountains towards Poprad. Just before Poprad, turn west on road no. 18, then north on road no. 534.

> ## Food and Drink 🍴
>
> ### ③ NOSTALGIE
> Letná 49, Spišská Nová Ves; tel: 053 441 4144; www.nostalgie.sk; €–€€
> Only a few minutes by car from Čingov, Spišská Nová Ves has a number of eating places, of which this one, on the town's stately main street, is the best. Nostalgic décor but innovative dishes.
>
> ### ④ HOTEL PRIEHRADA
> Dedinky; tel: 058 798 1212; €
> There are a number of refreshment opportunities around the car park serving the Dobšina Ice Cave, but probably the most pleasant place to eat in the area is back in Dedinky. Overlooking the lake, this hotel is the most sophisticated establishment in the settlement, with a café, restaurant and terrace.

Above from far left: couple standing on the edge of the Tomášov viewpoint; entrance to the Dobšina Ice Cave.

THE FAR EAST

This day tour introduces you to what is possibly the most remote and unvisited part of Slovakia, the Carpathian borderlands adjoining Poland and Ukraine. Deeply marked by memories of both world wars, it nevertheless has charming little churches and is where Pop artist Andy Warhol was born.

Icons

The icons which are such a feature of the region's churches can also be viewed in a branch of Bardejov's museum, at the upper end of the main square (same times and charges as the local museum, *see right*).

DISTANCE 97km (60 miles)

TIME A full day

START Bardejov

END Medzilaborce

POINTS TO NOTE

Both Bardejov (76km/47 miles north of the eastern Slovak capital of Košice) and Medzilaborce are at the end of branch railway lines, and all the places described are served by buses. But to get the most out of this itinerary, especially if you want to visit more than one or two timber churches, it really is vital to have your own car. The timber churches along the route are usually locked, but details of key-holders are easy to find. Look for a notice on the church door or ask around.

You begin in Bardejov, one of the country's most exquisite historic towns, then head eastwards through a sombre landscape relieved by the presence of the tiny timber churches characteristic of the region. The day concludes with the surprise of a museum devoted to the Pop artist Andy Warhol.

BARDEJOV

A candidate for the title of best-preserved small historic town in Slovakia, **Bardejov ❶** has a spacious central square lined with burghers' houses, a perfect setting for its great Gothic church and Renaissance Town Hall. Well away from today's main traffic routes, it is a place to linger and slowly absorb the pervasive sense of the distant past. The town's history has not been an uneventful one. The original

settlement was devastated when the Mongols swept through in 1241, but was then rebuilt by German settlers to become an important trading centre, whose golden age came in the 15th century. Formidable town walls, much of which still stand, are evidence of further troubled times, and fires and plagues accelerated Bardejov's decline. By the middle of the 20th century, few of the town's German population remained to be expelled, and almost all of its sizeable Jewish population perished in the Holocaust.

Church of St Egidius

The **Church of St Egidius** (Kostol sv. Egídia; Mon–Fri 9.30am–4.30pm, Sat 10am–3pm, Sun 11.30am–2pm; charge) dominates the northern end of the gently sloping square. Its sheer size and the richly furnished interior – including nearly a dozen late Gothic altarpieces – are impressive evidence of the town's wealth in the early 15th century. It is well worth paying the entrance fee simply to climb to the top of the tower for the superlative view over the town in its setting of rolling hills.

Bardejov Town Hall

Down in the square again, the steep-roofed **Town Hall** (Radnica) was started as a Gothic structure in the early 16th century, but has many early Renaissance features thanks to the Italian craftsmen who also worked on it; these include a lovely external staircase. A statue of the knight Roland graces the top of one high gable, while a less elegant character exposes his naked

posterior to all those who enter the building, possibly the work of a sculptor refused his rightful fee. The Town Hall now houses a branch of the local **Šariš Museum (Šarišské múzeum;** May–Sept: daily 8.30am–noon, 12.30–4.30pm, Oct–Apr: Tue–Sun 8.30am–4pm; charge) dealing with Bardejov's history up to the 18th century. The most appealing items are the medieval religious sculptures, among them a work by Master Paul *(see p.69).*

When it is time to eat, head for **El**, see ①, or **Bellevue**, see ②.

BARDEJOVSKÉ KÚPELE

Despite its seemingly remote location, Bardejov has attracted visitors from all over Europe and beyond for some time, though many tended to bypass the town itself and go on to take the waters at **Bardejovské Kúpele ②**, the spa town 4.5km (3 miles) to the north. Like other Slovak spas, it has a park-like character, with the medical installations, hotels and other facilities laid out along a well-

Above from far left: Bardejov's glorious architecture; fine icons at the town's local museum.

Jewish Bardejov
The life of Bardejov's Jewish community focused on a compound just to the west of the historic centre. The centrepiece of the compound – now used as a storage yard for a building materials company – is a splendid but dilapidated early 19th-century synagogue, complete with a *mikvah,* a ritual bath.

Food and Drink

① EL
Stöcklova 43, Bardejov; tel: 054 472 3338; €
Pleasant town-centre restaurant one street away from the main square, with vegetarian dishes and salads as well as the usual Slovak and international fare. Outside terrace.

② BELLEVUE
Mihal'ov 2503, Bardejov; tel: 054 472 8404; www.bellevuehotel.sk; €€–€€€
If you have already spent the night at the Bellevue, you may be tempted to take a break from sightseeing and drive up the hill again to enjoy a well-prepared, impeccably served gourmet repast, possibly featuring vegetables grown on the hotel's own plot.

Sissi

In Bardejovské kúpele, do not miss the elegant statue of slim-waisted 'Sissi', Emperor Franz Josef's wife Elizabeth (1837–98). Monarchs and their consorts found little favour in this part of the world after the fall of Austria-Hungary in 1918, and even less so under Communism; Bardejov's Sissi has only been saved from being broken up by judiciously changing her name on several occasions; for a while she represented a banker's wife, then the 'ideal of Slovak womanhood'. Her true identity has now been restored.

landscaped valley. The spa town has gone down rather in the world since its glory days before World War I, when it was patronised by kings and emperors; nowadays, people come here to be cured of digestive and respiratory problems rather than to see and be seen, but the surroundings are still pleasant, and, as a place to stay, it is a good alternative to Bardejov itself.

Open-Air Museum

The spa has its own *skanzen,* the **Open-Air Museum** (Múzeum ľudovej architektúry; May–Sept: daily 8.30am–6pm, Oct–Apr: Tue–Sun 8am–noon, 12.30–4pm), with several dozen traditional timber buildings typical of the region. If lack of time prevents you from driving around the area 'church spotting', there are two examples here of timber churches (one outside the *skanzen).*

HERVATOV

If you have been taken by the idea of visiting some of the region's timber churches, there is a fine example in the village of **Hervatov** ❸, 8km (5 miles) south of Bardejov. Leave town on road no. 545 in the direction of Prešov,

turning right after 5km (3 miles) in Kľušovská Zábava, then left after 1km (½ mile). Prettily sited above a brook in the middle of the village, this wooden church is unusual in that it is exceptionally old – originally built in the 16th century – and that it serves a Roman Catholic congregation. The interior is particularly fascinating, with colourful wall-paintings of such subjects as St George and the Dragon, Adam and Eve, and the Wise and Foolish Virgins.

SVIDNÍK AND THE DUKLA

To continue the tour, drive northeast from Bardejov or Bardejovské Kúpele on road no. 77 towards **Svidník** ❹. With a sad, even tragic history, this rather nondescript town with a majority Ruthene population is not at first sight a place you might want to linger in.

Always poor, in the early 20th century it lost much of its population to emigration, then in both world wars was right on the front line. Burned to the ground by the retreating Austro-Hungarian army in 1915, in 1944 the town and the country around was the scene of months of bitter fighting as the Wehrmacht tried to prevent the Red Army breaking through the natural barrier of the Carpathians.

The whole area has consequently become a landscape of remembrance, with military memorials, cemeteries where thousands of soldiers are buried, and the **Military Museum (**Voyenské historické múzeum; July–Aug: Tue–Fri 8am–3.30pm, Sat–Sun 10am–5pm, Sept–June: Tue–Fri 8am–3.30pm, Sat–

Sun 10am–2pm; charge), with displays on the battles. Take road no. 73/E371 up to the **Dukla Pass ❺** (Dukliansky priesmyk) on the Slovak–Polish border, a highway littered with military hardware, including German and Soviet tanks seemingly locked in combat.

Timber Churches

Pause on the way if you have time to look at the timber churches in the villages of **Ladomirová**, **Hunkovce** and **Nižný Komárnik**. The first was built without the use of a single nail, the second is set among oaks and limes, and the third is a relatively modern structure, dating from only 1938.

Just before you reach the frontier post on the pass there is a large, sombre memorial to the Czechoslovak soldiers who fell here fighting alongside the Russians, as well as a 52m (170ft) high **lookout tower** (mid-May–mid-Oct: Tue–Sun; charge), giving a breathtaking panoramic view of the battlefield.

MEDZILABORCE

Resisting the temptation to drive on into Poland, go back the way you came, and in 6km (4 miles) turn left on to a minor road in the direction of Bodružal just before the village of Krajná Poľana. You pass through the villages of **Bodružal** and **Miroľa**, each with a delightful timber church, before reaching main road no. 575 near the village of Makovce, where you turn left and follow signs to **Medzilaborce ❻**. This otherwise unremarkable and remote small town lies at the centre

of the area from which the Ruthenian Varhola clan sprang.

Andy Warhol Museum

The Varhola family honour their most illustrious offspring with the **Andy Warhol Museum (**Múzeum Andyho Warhola; Tue–Fri 10am–4pm, Sat–Sun noon–4pm; charge), a modern building guarded by oversized examples of the Campbell's soup cans made famous by the artist (one doubles up as a bus shelter). Inside there is a selection of works by members of the family as well as by the master himself, among them his Pop-Art interpretations of Communist icons such as Lenin. After the visit, the **Penzión Andy**, see ⓷, is the best place to stop for a bite.

There is not much else to detain you in Medzilaborce, which, like Svidník, suffered a battering in both world wars. One building you cannot fail to notice is the prominent Orthodox church in traditional Ukrainian style, built, surprisingly enough, in the early years of the Communist regime.

Above from far left: stripes and Pop Art portraits of Andy Warhol at Medzilaborce's museum dedicated to his work.

Eastern Slovakia's Wooden Churches All along this part of the Slovak/Polish/ Ukrainian borderland there are dozens of timber churches. Mostly dating from the 18th century, they are masterpieces of the carpenter's art, while their interiors are often richly furnished with icons and wall-paintings. The churches often stand on elevated ground, surrounded by trees. Some have simple roofs, others have elaborate onion domes reflecting the building's internal layout.

'The Man from Nowhere'

Andy Warhol (1928–87) was characteristically elusive about his roots, declaring famously that he 'came from nowhere'. In fact he was a product of the industrial city of Pittsburgh, Pennsylvania, to where his father and mother had emigrated from poverty-stricken Slovakia in the years before World War I. Brought up to speak Ruthenian as well as English, Andy never professed any interest in his ancestral land, and it was only after his death that his brother and other members of the Varhola family opened a museum dedicated to him in the far-off Carpathian foothills.

KOŠICE

An introductory stroll around the historic centre of the lively capital of eastern Slovakia, taking in its stunning Gothic cathedral, a main art gallery and some great spots for people-watching.

Above: strolling through central Košice; the city's Jesuit Church.

Athletic City

Košice is proud of its marathon, run since 1924 and thus Europe's oldest, and of Martina Hingisová, the tennis prodigy born here in 1980.

Right: detail of the plague column.

DISTANCE 1km (½ mile)
TIME From one hour up to a full day, depending on how long you spend perusing the city's galleries and museums
START Košice main rail and bus stations
END Plague Column
POINTS TO NOTE
Probably the best way to tackle Košice is to spend the morning strolling and orientating yourself (climbing the cathedral tower, *see p.84,* will help), and the afternoon visiting museums and galleries of your choice.

Some 400km (248 miles) east of Bratislava, Košice is an important communications hub, well served by rail and by long-distance coach services. Consequently this walking tour begins at the main rail and bus stations, and takes you along the broad and lengthy boulevard-cum-square that runs from one end of the historic core to the other.

A BUZZING CITY

Especially if you have been touring eastern Slovakia, you will be struck by Košice's big-city atmosphere, certainly compared with the provincial character of most of the region's towns. The scale of the buildings, the animation of the people thronging the streets, the mixture of languages (there are substantial Hungarian and Roma minorities) give the city a buzz otherwise only found in the capital, Bratislava.

History

Košice has always been special; founded in the 13th century astride important trading routes, it soon prospered, becoming the second-largest city in the Hungarian kingdom. But its greatest expansion came relatively recently, after World War II, when the Communist regime boosted it as an industrial centre,

Above from far left:
Košice's main square;
Hotel Slavia sign;
window-shoppers.

mainly by making it the site of the gargantuan East Slovak Ironworks, now owned by a US corporation. Despite this smokestack heritage, the old centre has retained its character, which was greatly enhanced during the second period of office (1994–9) of mayor Rudolf Schuster, who later became the country's president (1999–2004). Traffic was banned, tasteful paving was laid, and features were provided like the water channel along the middle of Hlavná, a reminder of the brook that once flowed here.

EXPLORING KOŠICE

Along with Košice's central park, the **bus and railway stations ❶** are situated just to the east of the historic centre, in an area just outside the old city walls which were demolished in the 19th century. Head west along a pedestrian walkway that crosses over the ring road which occupies the line of an old river. On your right stands the late 19th-century **Jakabov Palace ❷** (Jakabov palác), a fantastical neo-Gothic apartment block with a corner

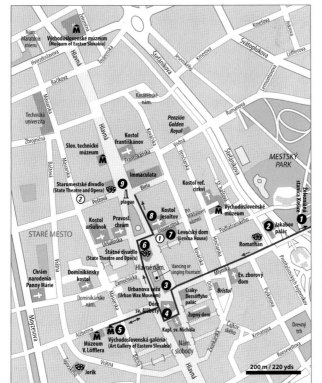

Horsepower

Electric trams form the backbone of public transport in Košice, but since pedestrianisation took place they have been banned from the main square. The lines have been kept, however, and in summer they are used for nostalgic trips aboard a horse-drawn tram.

Cathedral Details
If you look up carefully
at the cathedral's
unfinished south
tower, you should be
able to make out the
gargoyle popularly
called the 'drunken
woman', supposedly
carved by a sculptor
fed up with his wife's
boozy habits. Take
note, also, of the
fine stained-glass
windows, details
of which are
shown above.

tower, built partly with damaged
stonework salvaged from the cathedral
in the late 19th century. Continue
westwards along Mlynská until you
reach **Hlavná**, Košice's extraordinarily
long, spindle-shaped central artery.

On to Hlavná

Directly in front of you as the square
opens up is a medieval civic bell tower,
which is now home to the **Urban Wax
Museum** ❸ (Urbanova veža; Tue–Sun
noon–4pm; free). To the right is one of
Schuster's improvements, the '**dancing
or singing fountain**', which performs
hourly, accompanied by the chimes of
a carillon.

Cathedral of St Elizabeth

In the post-Communist era, Košice's
pride is not so much the East Slovak
Ironworks as the **Cathedral of St
Elizabeth** ❹ (Dom sv. Alžbety; daily
5.30am–7pm; free), which completely

dominates this part of the square.
Begun in the late 14th century, the
cathedral is the largest and most beautiful building of its type in Slovakia, as
well as the easternmost outpost of the
Gothic style in the whole of Europe,
and it repays a leisurely visit, both inside
and out. The exterior is richly ornamented with sculpture, while inside, the
finest feature is probably the exquisite
double staircase, a masterpiece of late
medieval workmanship.

You can descend into the depths of
the **crypt**, especially built to house the
remains of one of the great heroes of
Hungarian history, Ferenc Rákóczi,
or climb up the **tower** (both Mon–Fri
9.30am–4.30pm, Sat 9.30am–1.30pm;
charge) for an all-round view of the
city in its setting.

Back at ground level, go round to the
far side of the cathedral, where a landscaped garden that was once a cemetery is watched over by a little chapel
dedicated to St Michael.

Art Gallery of Eastern Slovakia

Opposite, on the eastern side of the
square, is one of many palaces in the
vicinity of Hlavná, now the home of
the **Art Gallery of Eastern Slovakia**
❺ (Východoslovenská galéria; Tue–Fri
10am–5.30pm, Sat 1–5.30pm, Sun 2–
5.30pm; charge). This has one of the
more rewarding art collections in the
country, and is particularly rich in early
20th-century painting.

The building has a notable history:
in early 1945, when Košice was the only
major city in Czechoslovakia to have
been liberated by the Red Army, the

gallery served briefly as the headquarters of the Czechoslovak government on its return from exile in London.

Other Sights on the Hlavná

Now walk back past the cathedral and admire the much later edifice also occupying a central position in the square. This is the **Štátné divadlo** ❻ (State Theatre and Opera), a pompous structure built at the very end of the 19th century and in no way inferior to its counterpart in Bratislava. On the east side of the square, building no. 65, one of Košice's most attractive Art Nouveau structures, houses a city institution, the **Kaviáreň Slavia**, see ⑪①.

Sharing the same number is the venerable **Levoča House** ❼ (Levočský dom) of 1542, the Košice base in late medieval times of merchants from the town of Levoča, with a pub/restaurant that has been in continuous operation ever since its foundation. Further along on the same side of the square, the rather grim façade of the **Jesuit Church** ❽ (Kostol jesuitov) in sombre grey stone belies its Baroque interior, where stunning *trompe l'œil* paintings enhance the elaborate décor. In the centre of the square, a **plague column** ❾ rises from an attractively gardened area, a pleasant spot to recuperate and contemplate your next move. For refreshment, **Dobrá Čajovňa**, see ⑪②, is nearby.

Coin Collection

Košice's main street is terminated to the north by the buildings of the Museum of Eastern Slovakia (Východoslovenská múzeum), whose prize exhibit is the Košice Gold Hoard, an extraordinary collection of 3,000 gold coins stashed away and only recovered in the course of building work in the 1930s.

Left: Košice's main street.

WEST FROM KOŠICE

This circular tour leads through the countryside of the Slovak Ore Mountains before dropping to the lowlands by the border with Hungary. Near the ancient mining town of Rožňava are a hilltop stronghold and an elaborate hunting lodge, relics of one of the aristocratic dynasties of the Hungarian kingdom.

Medzev Smithies

Medzev was famous for the quality of its ironwork, with at one time more than 100 water-powered smithies at work. A preserved example stands by the road-side on the right as you leave the village.

Below: Premonstratensian Monastery, Jasov.

DISTANCE 160km (99 miles)

TIME A full day

START/END Košice

POINTS TO NOTE

There are coach tours from Košice to the former Andrássy properties and regular bus and rail services to Rožnava, but the outward part of this tour is only possible using your own transport. For details on how to hire a car, *see p.105.*

Drive southwest from Košice on main road no. 50/E571 in the direction of Rožňava, turning right shortly after leaving the built-up area on to road no. 548. In 20km (12 miles) you will reach the small town of Jasov.

JASOV

On the eastern edge of the Slovenské rudohorie (Slovak Ore mountains), **Jasov** boasts its own set of limestone caves, though for the moment aim for the **Premonstratensian Monastery** ❶ (Premonštrátský klástor; access dependent on the whims of the white-robed monks, or try telephoning 090 363 2606 to arrange a visit in advance). The monastery dates from the 12th

Food and Drink 🍴

① U ŽELEZNÉHO GRÓFA

Tichá ul. 635, Krásnohorské Podhradie; tel: 058 732 9980; €

Visible from main road no. 50 on the eastern edge of Krásnohorské Podhradie, the 'Iron Count' is a cheerful, well-run restaurant in an immaculate new building. As well as the usual range of Slovak comestibles, there are daily specials, and if you are lucky there will be roast goose liver among them. Vegetarians are catered for as well.

century, but was lavishly rebuilt in the 18th century as an eastern outpost of Viennese Baroque style. The interior of the twin-towered church is sumptuously decorated with illusionistic wall-paintings, as is the magnificent library. To the rear of the complex is a large formal garden with exotic trees.

From Jasov, continue northwest on road no. 548, which runs past Roma settlements towards the old industrial village of **Medzev**. Medzev once had a mostly German population, their most famous offspring being ex-president Schuster *(see p.83)*.

THE ORE MOUNTAINS

At the village of Štós, the road begins to climb up into the well-forested **Slovak Ore mountains** (Slovenské rudohorie). Before reaching the summit, turn left to **Štós Spa ②** (Štós kúpele), a low-key establishment scattered among the trees, and famed for sitting among what is claimed to be the purest air in the country. The main building has a café/restaurant, a possible refreshment stop.

About 2km (just over 1 mile) beyond the forested summit, interrupt your descent and stop by a chapel on the left for a fine view down to the old German mining town of **Smolník ③** in its lovely upland setting. The sheer size of Smolník's parish church is testimony to the place's former prosperity, the source of which is commemorated on the green below the church, where a wagon containing the last ton of iron to be extracted makes a rather mournful memorial.

Krásna Hôrka Castle

From Smolník, road no. 549, narrow, winding and poorly maintained in parts, climbs over the mountains towards Rožňava and Krásnohorské Podhradie, the village below the hilltop castle of Krásna Hôrka. The castle is poorly signposted when approached from this direction; watch out for a turning to the right 2km (just over 1 mile) short of the village. Alternatively, if it feels like time for a break, continue into the village where there is a good restaurant, **U Železného Grófa**, see ⓪①.

After the pause, drive back the way you came and turn left through the woods to the castle car park. Leave your vehicle in the car park and climb on foot to **Krásna Hôrka Castle ④** (Hrad

Above from far left: Jasov; painted ceiling in the Premonstratensian Monastery, Jasov.

Above: view from the castle walls, Krásna Hôrka; iron-ore wagon, Jasov.

Magyar Menus
Before World War II, Rožňava had a majority Hungarian population. Even today more than a quarter of its citizens are Hungarian-speakers, and the town and its surroundings attract plenty of tourists and day trippers from across the border. Do not be surprised to find menus and other information written in Hungarian as well as Slovak.

Krásna Hôrka; Tue–Sun, May–Oct: 8.30am–4.30pm, Nov–Apr: 9am–2.30pm; charge). One of the many properties of the powerful Andrássy family, the castle was strengthened in the 16th century to withstand attack from the Turkish occupiers of the Hungarian plains to the south. It is well stocked with furniture, family memorabilia and weaponry. In 1910 it was turned into a museum and opened to the public by one of the more unconventional Andrássys, Count Dionysus, who was disowned by his family for marrying a commoner, the Czech opera singer Františka Hablavcová.

Andrássy Mausoleum
In 1904, following Františka's death, Dionysus built her a magnificent resting place, the **Andrássy Mausoleum** ❺ (Mauzóleum Andrássyovcov; Tue–Sun, May–Oct: 8am–5.30pm, Nov–Apr: 9am–3pm; charge; take care in parking at the side of this fast and busy road and cross with care). Just to the east of Krasnohorska Podhradie on main road

no. 50, the mausoleum is as opulent an example of Art Nouveau as Jasov's monastery is of the Baroque, with lavish use of materials such as gold and marble.

ROŽŇAVA

Go back the way you have just come on road no. 50 to the fine old mining town of **Rožňava** ❻, 7km (4 miles) further west along the main road. Even here there is a reminder of the Andrássy family's massive imprint on the region, a statue of the much-loved Františka. She stands in the almost perfectly square-shaped central square, next to the town's symbol, the 17th-century **Watchtower** (Strážna veža; July–Aug: Mon–Fri 10am–5.30pm, Sat 10am–3.30pm, Sun noon–3.30pm, Sept–June: Mon–Fri 10am, 11am, 1pm and 2pm, otherwise by arrangement; charge). Climb to the top for a fine panorama over the town, which was founded by German miners in the 13th century. On the fault line between the Habsburg lands and Turkish-occupied Hungary,

Darling 'Dachsie'
Look behind the main building of the Andrássy Mausoleum for the poignant memorial to little 'Tascherl', the Count's favourite dachshund.

Rožňava was devastated on more than one occasion, and its present harmonious appearance is largely due to its 18th-century rebuilding.

Mining Heritage

The most picturesque corner is where the northwestern edge of the square opens out towards the cathedral, which contains a real curiosity, a 16th-century painting of St Anne against a background of realistically depicted mining scenes. For anyone wanting to find out about the area's mining heritage, there is the **Mining Museum (**Banícke múzeum; Tue–Fri 8am–4pm; charge), which also has displays on the natural history of the limestone landscapes of the Slovak Karst (Slovenský kras), part of the Ore mountains.

BETLIAR

Head north out of Rožňava on road no. 67 towards Dobšiná, turning right after 5km (3 miles) and following signs to Kaštiel. Here is another Andrássy residence, **Betliar ❼** (Tue–Sun May–Oct: 8am–4.30pm, Nov–Apr: 9am–2pm; charge), this time not a castle but an opulent country house used mainly as a hunting lodge. It is lavishly furnished, giving a good impression of the life led not just by the Andrássys but by the aristocracy in general in the 18th and 19th centuries. Its lovely, extensive park is graced by garden buildings and by a whole range of exotic trees; it is one of the finest of its kind in Central Europe.

For a dining experience not quite Andrássy-style but pleasant enough, visit the **Penzión pri kaštieli Betliar**, see ⑪②, which is also in the grounds. You can make a rapid return to Košice by going back down to road no. 50, bypassing Rožňava.

Above from far left: sundial in Rožňava's main square; Andrássy Mausoleum; ornate door knocker at the Andrássy Mausoleum; colourful architecture in Rožňava.

Food and Drink 🍴

② **PENZIÓN PRI KAŠTIELI BETLIAR**
Kaštiel'na 16, Betliar; tel: 058 788 2002; €
If you are tempted to linger in the aristocratic surroundings of Betliar, you could do worse than join the crowds of visitors in this guesthouse close to the Andrássy residence. Its attractive and popular restaurant is located in what was once part of the mansion's stables.

Andrássy Family

One of the great noble families of Hungary, the Andrássy clan originated in Transylvania, though most of their vast holdings of land were in what is now Slovakia (once called 'Upper Hungary' by its rulers). As well as individualists like Dionysus, the family produced great statesmen, among them Gyula (1823–1890), prime minister of Hungary 1867–71, and his son, also Gyula (1860–1929), the very last foreign minister of Austria–Hungary.

DIRECTORY

A user-friendly alphabetical listing of practical information,
plus hand-picked hotels and restaurants, clearly organised
by area, to suit all budgets and tastes.

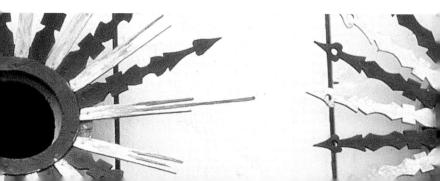

A

ADMISSION CHARGES

Virtually all museums and similar attractions in Slovakia have an entry charge, though this will be low by Western European standards. There are the usual reductions for children, and in some cases students (with student card) and senior citizens may also pay a reduced amount.

AGE RESTRICTIONS

The legal age for buying and consuming alcohol is 18. There is no set age limit for hiring a car, but individual rental firms may operate their own restrictions.

B

BUDGETING

Because wages, salaries and prices in this new member of the European Union (EU) are still comparatively low, a holiday in Slovakia can offer very good value indeed. However, this only applies if you do as local people do, staying in budget hotels or camping, travelling by public transport, eating in unpretentious restaurants or putting together a picnic, and avoiding places frequented by foreign visitors and the native business elite. Hotels and restaurants are noticeably more expensive in Bratislava than elsewhere in the country, but even here it is possible to live economically by keeping a close eye on your budget.

C

CHILDREN

Slovaks tend to be family-orientated and consequently well disposed and helpful towards child travellers, thereby making up for a certain lack in facilities designed specifically for youngsters.

With its wealth of natural attractions, the country itself is great for the active child, and in many ways is an ideal holiday destination for families looking for an open-air holiday. The possibilities of walking, climbing, rafting, observing wildlife, swimming in rivers and pools are all there in abundance.

Castles offer costumed spectacles and displays of falconry, and there are plenty of folkloric events too, often held in the regional open-air museums where there may also be farm animals to see and stroke, as well as demonstrations of traditional crafts.

Practicalities
Children are usually admitted to museums and other attractions at substantially reduced rates and enjoy half fares on public transport.

Babysitting services are only likely to be available in the more expensive establishments, but most hotels will provide children's beds and cots for a modest charge.

CLIMATE

Slovakia has a temperate climate with continental influences. This results in cold winters, while the warm summers

are frequently punctuated by rainfall. There are considerable variations according to elevation and latitude; Bratislava and the Danube lowlands are notably sunny, while snow can fall in the High Tatras at any time of the year. Climate change has in recent years yielded a succession of mild winters, confounding the expectations of skiers used to several months of reliable snow cover.

Prolonged sightseeing in towns can become an ordeal at the height of summer, and the best times for urban explorations are late spring, early summer, and early autumn. By contrast, high summer is the best time for walking in the mountains.

CLOTHING

Practical, casual clothing should suit most occasions, though a degree of smartness is appropriate if going to the opera, a classical concert, or an upmarket restaurant. Be prepared for summer showers with some sort of rainwear and take winter conditions seriously – as Slovaks typically do. Between November and March, warm coat, headgear and gloves are essential, not optional extras.

In the mountains, do note that climatic conditions deteriorate swiftly with altitude, and that the weather at the top of the funicular may be quite different from that in the valley. Note also that mountain walking requires boots, not trainers, plus waterproofs and a sweater in case of sudden drops in temperature.

CRIME AND SAFETY

Slovakia is generally a safe country to travel in as long as you take the normal precautions. Pickpocketing and thefts from cars are the principal threats, so carry valuables in inside pockets, keep bags close to your body, and do not leave anything on view in your car, which is best left in a secure car park rather than on the street. Avoid ill-lit streets at night. It is a good idea to note the numbers of credit cards and make a photocopy of your passport.

Visits by strangers to Roma settlements are likely to attract attention, which may seem threatening but is more likely to be an uninhibited expression of curiosity, often accompanied by requests for money.

CUSTOMS

There are restrictions on the amount of alcohol, tobacco and perfume visitors can bring into the country, but these regulations only seem to be applied loosely, and in any case such items or their equivalents can be bought locally at what are usually very reasonable prices. The export of valuable works of art or antiques requires a licence. Dealers will advise on how to arrange this.

Foreign visitors need a passport or, in the case of EU citizens entitled to one, an identity card. Visas are only necessary for visitors from certain countries; check with the local Slovak embassy if in doubt. Anyone planning an extended stay (usually more than 90 days) will require a resident's permit.

Above from far left: food and drinks are great value in Slovakia; traditionally dressed horse.

D

DISABLED TRAVELLERS

Little attention was paid in the past to the needs of disabled travellers, and the catching-up process has been slow. New and refurbished hotels and restaurants may well have acceptable access arrangements, others may not. Some long-distance trains have a coach with disabled access.

DRIVING

The road network is generally of a high standard. Main roads are well engineered and maintained, minor roads less so. The rather sparse motorway network is slowly being extended. Traffic can be heavy on main roads, and driving behaviour is sometimes erratic, notably on the part of local owners of expensive vehicles with blacked-out windows.

Road Signs

Slovak road signs are of the standard European type, and there is adequate directional signposting.

Parking

This can be difficult in larger towns. Note that local police are usually vigilant in enforcing regulations.

Petrol/Gas

The country is well supplied with filling stations. On main routes some are open 24/7; many house mini-supermarkets. Fuel prices are somewhat lower than in most Western European countries.

Documents/Legalities

Drivers must be in possession of a valid driving licence, and vehicles must be insured. If you bring your own car you must have proof of possession, fix a national identity sticker to the rear of the vehicle, and carry a red breakdown triangle, spare light bulbs, tow rope and first aid kit. To drive on motorways you must purchase and display a sticker, valid for various periods and obtainable at frontier crossings and filling stations.

Seat belts must be worn, and small children may not sit in the front of the vehicle. Headlights must be switched on (dipped) when driving in winter, and in fact most drivers have them on at all times. There is zero tolerance for driving with any alcohol at all in the bloodstream.

Speed Limits

The speed limit on motorways is 130kph (80mph), 90kph (55mph) on other roads and 60kph (37mph) in built-up areas – which are indicated by the place-name sign. Beware that these limits are regularly ignored by many Slovak drivers, although we certainly do not commend this.

E

ELECTRICITY

Electricity is supplied at 220/230 volts and appliances are connected by two-pin plugs of the standard continental type. British three-pin appliances will need an adaptor.

EMBASSIES

Australia: There is no embassy in Slovakia. Australians should contact the Australian embassy in Vienna at: Mattiellistraße 2, Vienna 1040, Austria; tel: +43 (0) 1 506 740; www. austria.embassy.gov.au.

Canada: The actual embassy is located in Prague, but it has a Bratislava office at: Carlton Savoy Building, Mostová 2, 811 02 Bratislava; tel: 02 5920 4031; www.canada.cz.

Ireland: Carlton Savoy Building, Mostová 2, 811 02 Bratislava; tel: 02 5930 9611.

New Zealand: There is no embassy in Slovakia. New Zealand nationals should contact the New Zealand Embassy in Berlin at: Atrium, Friedrichstrasse 60, 10117 Berlin, Germany; tel: 49 30 206 210; www.nz embassy.com.

UK: Panská 16, 811 01 Bratislava; tel: 02 5998 2000; www.britishembassy.sk.

US: Hviezdoslavovo námestie 5, 811 02 Bratislava; tel: 02 5443 0861/3338; http://slovakia.usembassy.gov.

EMERGENCIES

Emergency telephone numbers are as follows:
Police: 158
Ambulance: 155
Fire brigade: 150

ETIQUETTE

Racism: Unfortunately 'non-PC' remarks and behaviour are common-place, particularly concerning the Roma minority. If mistaken for Roma, dark-skinned visitors from other countries might find themselves treated unpleasantly; when the error is realised, normal Slovak hospitality will take over, but this will likely shock some visitors who are used to more enlightened attitudes.

F

FESTIVALS

Music, dance, folklore and wine form the backbone of the Slovak festival calendar, and visitors are likely to encounter some sort of festivity whenever and wherever they find themselves here. In summer, there is almost always something folkloric going on in the many open-air museums, while many castles, even ruined ones, stage some sort of historical pageant, with costumed performers, swordfights, mock battles, falconry and the like.

February
Štrbské Pleso: 'driving winter out' folklore spectacle.

April
Pezinok: Wine market.

May
Bojnice Castle: International Ghosts and Spirits festival.

July
Detva: Major folk music festival.
Levoča: Slovakia's most popular pilgrimage in honour of the Virgin Mary.

Východná: The country's largest folk music festival.

August
Terchová: Jánošík Days folk festival.
High Tatras: mass climb to the summit of Kriváň.

September
Bratislava: Colourful restaging of historic coronation ceremony.
Pezinok/Modra: Wine harvest festival.
Banská Štiavnica: Salamander Days celebration of mining traditions.

September–October
Bratislava: Bratislava music festival, a major classical music event spanning over two weeks.

October
Bratislava: Jazz festival.
Košice: International Peace marathon.

November
Pezinok: Open Cellars Day wine-tasting.

December
Bratislava: Christmas market.

FURTHER READING

Slovak Fiction

Contemporary Slovak literature is alive and well, though hardly any of its riches have been translated into English. An exception is Peter Pišťánek's *Rivers of Babylon* trilogy, whose hero Rajz – 'a vulgar, unstoppable idiot of genius' – thrives in the 'bare-knuckled capitalism' of post-Communist Slovakia.

Non-Fiction

The following is a list of recommended non-fiction titles:

Abelovský J., *Art in Changing Times – Painting & Sculpture in Slovakia 1890–1949* (Popelka-Slovart 2000). A beautifully illustrated doorstopper.

Bardwell S., *Tatra Mountains of Poland and Slovakia* (Sunflower Books 2006). Drives and walks on both sides of the frontier, in the Low Tatras and Slovak Paradise as well as the High Tatras.

Catchpole P., *Steam and Rail in Slovakia* (Locomotives International 1998). Enthusiastic introduction to the world of Slovak trains by British railfan.

Dowling M., *Czechoslovakia* (Arnold 2002). Authoritative paperback introduction to the making and breaking of Czechoslovakia.

Henderson K., *Slovakia – the Escape from Invisibility* (Routledge 2002). Political scientist's analysis of how Slovakia asserted its own identity before, during and after the break-up of Czechoslovakia.

Hochberger E., Kállay K., *Wonders of Slovakia* (Ikar 2003). Probably the best picture book on Slovakia, with great photographs and evocative text.

Kirschbaum S., *A History of Slovakia – the Struggle for Survival* (Palgrave Macmillan 2005). US Slovak's patriotic account of the nation's evolution.

Kliment C., Nakládal B., *Germany's First Ally – Armed Forces of the Slovak State 1939–1945* (Schiffer 1997). Military historians describe in exhaustive detail the role of Slovakia's forces in World War II, including the Slovak National Uprising of 1944.

Lackova I., *A False Dawn: My Life as a Gypsy Woman in Slovakia* (University of Hertfordshire 2000). Personal account of how Communism tried and failed to integrate the Roma community.

Leigh-Fermor P., *A Time of Gifts* (John Murray 1977). Exuberant description of a young man's walk across Europe before World War II, including a stay in Bratislava.

Podolák P., *The Malá Fatra Mountains* (Dajama 2002). One of a series ('Knapsacked Travel in Slovakia') of poorly translated but very thorough guides to all popular walking areas in the country.

Saunders C., Nárožná R., *The High Tatras* (Cicerone 1994). Reliable guidebook for serious mountain walkers.

Seton-Watson R.W., *A History of the Czechs and Slovaks* (Hutchinson 1943). Definitive history by the British journalist instrumental in bringing the plight of Hungarian-ruled Slovaks to the attention of the world in the years before World War I.

Shawcross W., *Dubček* (Touchstone 1990). Biography of the Prague Spring politician who longed for 'Socialism with a human face' and who is probably the most internationally famous Slovak of all time.

Spiesz A., *Illustrated Slovak History – A Struggle for Sovereignty in Central Europe* (2002). Richly illustrated, comprehensive but controversial account.

Strhan M., *Slovakia and the Slovaks – A Concise Encyclopedia* (Goldpress 1994). Everything you ever wanted to know about the country and its inhabitants.

Wetzler A., *Escape from Hell: the Story of the Auschwitz Protocol* (Berghahn 2007). Together with a fellow Slovak Jew, in 1944, escapee Alfred Wetzler brought a largely indifferent world's attention to what was actually happening in Auschwitz.

G

GOVERNMENT

Since the fall of Communism in 1989 the Slovak Republic has been a parliamentary democracy. It has a president elected for a five-year term, and a prime minister who must command a majority of the 150 members of the single-chamber National Council (Parliament).

The balance of power between president and prime minister has fluctuated over the years; in the mid-1990s there was great friction between president Michal Kováč and the prime minister Vladimír Mečiar because of the latter's authoritarian stance and unscrupulous ruling style which threatened to derail the country's progress towards Nato and EU membership. From 1998, a new centre-right government eased the situation, and in 2004 Slovakia became a member of both organisations. With numerous political parties ranging from Communists to ultra-rightists, multi-party coalition governments have become the norm.

Since 2006 the country has been governed by an unusual combination of Robert Fico's SMER, which presents itself as a social-democratic party, Mečiar's nationalist HZDS movement, and the far-right Slovak National Party.

baltím a severnou Európou. Na
prihlého regiónu. Dnešný
a dôležité karpatské priesmyk

For local government purposes, Slovakia is divided into eight regions *(kraj)*, which are subdivided into 79 districts *(okres)* and 2,885 communities *(obec)*. The regional capitals are Bratislava, Trnava, Nitra, Trenčín, Žilina, Banská Bystrica, Prešov and Košice.

H

HEALTH CARE

The standard of health care in Slovakia is generally good, and visitors from other countries who are unlucky enough to fall ill should be well looked after. Emergency medical treatment is free of charge, though medicines may have to be paid for.

Before travelling, British subjects should obtain the European Health Insurance Card by completing the form obtainable at post offices, online at www.ehic.org.uk, or by telephoning 0845-606 2030.

Citizens of countries outside the EU should ensure that they have private health insurance, which is recommended for all travellers to cover the costs of any longer-term problems and to ensure repatriation if necessary. A pharmacy *(lékáreň)* can often help with minor health problems.

Ticks

Ticks can be a hazard in several Central European countries, including Slovakia. To avoid trouble, particularly when walking among trees and high grass, make sure your arms and legs are well covered, and in the unlikely event

of a tick embedding itself in your skin, remove it carefully with tweezers. Make sure that the head has not been left behind, since that may cause infection.

I

INTERNET

There are internet cafés in most towns, and the more expensive hotels have internet facilities.

L

LANGUAGE

Áno Yes
Nie No
Prosím Please
Dakujem Thank you
Prosím You are welcome
Niet za co Not at all
Prepáčte Sorry
Ahoj, cau Hello, Hi
Dovidenia Goodbye
Prepáčte , hovoríte po anglicky?
Excuse me, do you speak English?
Rozumiete? Do you understand?
Kde je (toaleta)? Where is (the toilet)?
Nerozumiem (po slovensky)
I do not understand (Slovak).
Mohli by ste mi/nam pomoct?
Could you help me/us?
Koľko to stojí? How much is it?

Numbers
Nula zero
Jeden one
Dva two
Tri three

este dnešného hradu stálo v obdot
ad vznikol v 11. storočí ako pohra
cez ktoré prechádzali obchodné c

Štyri four
Päť five
Šesť six
Sedem seven
Osem eight
Deväť nine
Desať ten
Jedenásť eleven
Dvanásť twelve
Pätnásť fifteen
Dvadsať twenty
Tridsať thirty
Štyridsať forty
Päťdesiat fifty
Šesťdesiat sixty
Sedemdesiat seventy
Osemdesiat eighty
Deväťdesiat ninety
Sto hundred
Dvesto two hundred
Tisíc thousand

Days of the Week
Pondelok Monday
Utorok Tuesday
Streda Wednesday
Štvrtok Thursday
Piatok Friday
Sobota Saturday
Nedeľa Sunday

LEFT LUGGAGE

Larger railway stations have lockers or left-luggage offices.

LOST PROPERTY

Larger railway stations may have a lost-property office. Elsewhere, visit the local police station for help.

M

MAPS

The VKÚ (Military Cartographic Institute), the Slovak equivalent of the British Ordnance Survey, publishes maps of the highest quality at 1:50 000 scale for the whole country, as well as beautifully detailed 1:25 000 maps of popular hiking areas such as the High Tatras, the Malá Fatra mountains and the Slovak Paradise. The Institute's Detailed Motoring Atlas *(Podrobný Autoatlas)* at 1:100 000 scale is also of a very high standard, despite its low price. Basic city plans are often provided free of charge by tourist information centres.

MEDIA

Press
Slovakia has a lively press landscape, with a full range of daily newspapers from serious publications to sensational 'boulevard' red-tops. Current affairs and cultural listings are dealt with in English by the *Slovak Spectator,* a well-established weekly published in Bratislava. The *Spectator* also publishes *Spectacular Slovakia*, an annual tourist guide to the whole country, with interesting feature articles as well as practical information. Outside of Bratislava, do not expect to find any English-language newspapers.

Television
Local public and private TV stations provide a very bland diet of dubbed

Above: Slovak sign, Trenčín Castle.

Hollywood films, thrillers and soaps. Hotel televisions normally receive several foreign satellite channels, often including CNN, and, more rarely, Sky and BBC News 24.

Radio

Slovak Radio International broadcasts a daily half-hour round-up of local information in English at 4.30pm on 5930 and 6055kHz in the medium waveband.

MONEY

Currency

The national currency is the Slovak *koruna* (crown, Sk for short), theoretically divided into 100 worthless *halier* (hellers). Coins come in denominations of 50 hellers, 1, 2, 5 and 10 crowns. Banknotes range in value from 20, 50, 100, 200, 500 and 1,000 to 5,000 crowns. Slovakia aims to enter the Euro zone in the near future, and some prices (e.g. in hotels and restaurants) are already posted in euros.

Recent approximate exchange rates:
£1 = Sk38
$1 = Sk20
€1 = Sk30

Banks

There is a choice of banks, including savings banks, in most towns in Slovakia, nearly all of which have exchange facilities for cash or travellers' cheques. It may pay to compare exchange rates and commission charges before making a transaction. Banking hours are normally 9am–5pm Mon–Fri.

Credit Cards

Major credit cards are widely accepted in areas frequented by visitors from abroad, less so in remote areas and in smaller establishments.

Cash Machines

Most banks have cash machines, use of which has become the most convenient way of withdrawing money. Check up on charges before leaving home, as banks have widely differing rates.

O

OPENING HOURS

Shops normally open 8am–6pm Monday to Friday and 9am–1pm Saturday, but shops in malls and supermarkets stay open late on Thursdays and some supermarkets never close.

Nearly all museums and historic buildings shut on Mondays; normal opening hours are Tuesday to Sunday 9 or 10am to 5pm, possibly closing at lunchtime. Many castles and open-air museums close down for the winter (Sept/Oct–Mar).

POLICE

The various Slovak police forces (national = *národná polícia*; municipal = *městská polícia*; traffic = *dopravná polícia*) have improved their formerly poor image in recent years. Nowadays, they are generally polite and helpful to foreigners, but their inadequate level of pay may tempt them to extract unreasonable amounts in fines for minor offences such as driving just over the speed limit. In such cases, make sure that you demand a proper receipt, and, if this is refused, take the number of the officer in question and report them.

POST

All towns and some villages have a post office *(pošta)*, normally open 8am–5pm weekdays and on Saturday mornings. Poste-restante facilities are available in the larger towns. Stamps can also be bought at newsagents and tobacconists. Slovak letterboxes are coloured orange.

PUBLIC HOLIDAYS

New Year's Day: 1 January
Three Kings: 6 January
Good Friday: date varies
Easter Monday: date varies
Labour Day: 1 May
**Victory over Fascism/
  End of World War II**: 8 May
Day of Saints Cyril and Methodius:
  5 July
**Outbreak of the Slovak National
  Uprising**: 29 August
Constitution Day: 1 September
**Our Lady of Sorrows/Virgin Mary,
  Patron Saint of Slovakia**:
  15 September
All Saints' Day: 1 November
Velvet Revolution Day: 17 November
Christmas Eve: 24 December
Christmas Day: 25 December
St Stephen's Day: 26 December

R

RELIGION

Slovakia can be considered a Roman Catholic country, with more than two-thirds of the population declaring themselves Catholics. Religious observance is widespread, albeit rather less than in neighbouring Poland, and the pronouncements of bishops and priests are taken seriously. Numerous new church buildings have sprung up to serve the housing estates built in Communist, and officially atheistic, times.

In the east of the country there are substantial Greek Catholic and Orthodox congregations, but the most significant religious minority is formed by the Protestants of the Lutheran Evangelical Church. Although numbering only around 7 per cent of the population, this community has played an important role in the development of the country, in the past producing a disproportionate number of intellectuals, high officials and military officers.

T

TELEPHONES

Most payphones now take cards (rather than coins), available from post offices and newsagents; this makes them more convenient for making long-distance and international calls.

The modernised national network, Slovak Telekom, is supplemented by a number of additional operators. There are two mobile operators, T-MobileSK

Above from far left: Slovak money; postbox.

and Orange (Globetel) using GSM 900/1800, and cover is available except in the most remote areas.

Telephone Codes

Local area codes begin with 0, which is omitted when making calls to Slovakia (country code 00 421) from abroad. Omit the code when dialling within the local area. To make an international call from Slovakia, dial 00 followed by the country code (Great Britain 44, US and Canada 1). Calls made from your hotel room may be convenient but are usually charged at several times the normal rate.

TIME ZONES

Slovak observes Central European Time, one hour ahead of Greenwich Mean Time, and clocks are changed for daylight saving in winter.

TIPPING

A service charge is normally included in the bill for a meal, but it is customary to up the amount to the nearest round figure. If taxi drivers have been helpful, add 10 per cent. Hotel porters deserve a small sum per item of luggage carried, not more than Sk50 in total.

TOILETS

Public toilets are scarce and may be maintained in less than perfect condition. Filling stations often have surprisingly good facilities. Time your sightseeing for comfort stops in cafés and restaurants. There is often a nominal charge for using a toilet.

TOURIST INFORMATION

The national tourism office is SACR (Slovak Tourist Board), with a head office in Banská Bystrica and another in Bratislava. SACR is more concerned with policy than with providing help directly to visitors, but it has a useful website, www.sacr.sk.

Hotel receptionists can usually provide leaflets, maps and details of local events.

Tourist Office Abroad

Slovakia has official tourist information offices in the Netherlands, Germany, Austria, Poland and Russia, but not in Britain.

One of the best sources of information in the UK is: Czech and Slovak Tourist Centre, 16 Frognal Parade, Finchley Road, London NW3 5HG; tel: 020 7794 3263.

See page 105 for useful websites.

In Slovakia

Most towns in Slovakia have an official tourist information centre as well as travel agencies able to provide general information. The official tourist centres belong to the AICES (Association of Information Centres in Slovakia), and are listed on the website www.infoslovak.sk.

Bratislava's well-organised and helpful tourist information centre, BKIS, is in the Old Town at Klobučnicka 2; tel: 092 5441 5801.

TRANSPORT

Slovakia has a well-developed transport infrastructure, with many places accessible by rail and virtually all by bus. A flight is usually the most convenient and often the least expensive way of getting to Slovakia unless your starting point is one of the neighbouring countries. Internal air services are very limited, but if your time is short it could be worth while flying between Bratislava and Košice in the east of the country.

Bratislava Airport

Bratislava airport is approximately 9km (6 miles) to the east of the city centre and has the usual facilities in its modern arrival and departure terminals. The trip to and from the city centre by taxi takes under 20 minutes, while bus no. 61 runs between the airport and the main railway station at frequent intervals between 5am and 11pm with a journey time of around 25 minutes.

The airport is linked by direct flights to many European cities and to a limited number of intercontinental destinations. The principal operator is the locally based airline SkyEurope, whose flights include services to London Stansted, Manchester and Dublin. Dublin is also served by Ryanair (www.ryanair.com), whose other destinations include London Stansted and Nottingham East Midlands. Air Slovakia (www.airslovakia.sk) operates a direct flight to Birmingham. The most convenient transatlantic flights are probably those operated by Lufthansa (www.lufthansa.com), involving a change at Frankfurt.

Other Airports

Regional airports at Žilina, Sliáč (for Banská Bystrica), Poprad-Tatry (for the Tatra mountains) and Košice offer only a limited number of flights. Vienna's Schwechat airport, located to the east of the Austrian capital, is only about 55km (35miles) from Bratislava and is used by many travellers to Slovakia.

There is a much greater choice of flights, including direct flights to intercontinental destinations, from Vienna-Schwechat. Flights may also be at more convenient times. Schwechat can be reached in just over an hour by bus from Bratislava airport and city centre or just under one hour by taxi.

The only regular flights from regional airports are to Prague and from Košice to Bratislava, though the budget airport Sky Europe (www.skyeurope.com) operates a London Stansted–Poprad-Tatry flight.

Rail

The rail network in Slovakia is administered by ZSR (Railways of the Slovak Republic), while the trains themselves are run by ZSSK (Railway Company of the Slovak Republic). In conjunction with the railways of adjoining countries, ZSSK operates a number of international services. There are direct links to and from cities in Austria, Bulgaria, Croatia, the Czech Republic, Germany, Greece, Hungary, Poland, Russia and Ukraine.

Above from far left: Bratislava airport is east of the city centre; view from the Dukla Pass (see p.81).

International Travel: overnight trains on these routes normally have sleeping accommodation. A single change brings a number of other destinations, such as Paris, within reach. Bratislava is linked to Prague in under four hours by the high-speed Slovenská strela (Slovak Bullet), a tilting Pendolino train, and in summer there is an overnight Motorail service between Prague and Poprad (for the High Tatras). Travel from Britain will involve a number of changes and is really only worth considering for anyone stopping off at other points en route.

Within Slovakia: all main towns are linked by various types of fast train. These include EuroCity (EC), Inter-City (IC), Expres (Ex) and Rýchlik (R) in descending order of speed and comfort. Most but not all main lines are electrified, but much of the network remains single-track. Using the principal east–west line (the Northern Transversal), trains take five hours to connect Bratislava with Košice, travelling on a rather indirect route via Trnava, Trenčín, Žilina and Poprad (for the High Tatras). The infrequent service on what would appear to be a more direct Bratislava–Košice route through the centre of the country via Banská Bystrica takes nearly eight hours.

Branch lines are mostly served by stopping trains (Os), many of them consisting of boneshaking four-wheel diesel railbuses.

The **High Tatras** have their own electric railway, a kind of mountain super-tram giving panoramic views.

Services are generally reliable, and fares are low, making first-class travel an option worth considering. You may need to purchase a seat reservation on some long-distance services. For timetable information visit: www. slovakrail.sk (in Slovak only) or www. cd.cz (Czech railways website, which also gives Slovak train information, in English).

Coach Travel

International Travel: the Eurolines network links Slovakia by comfortable and well-equipped coaches to a number of countries, including Austria, Britain, the Czech Republic, France, Germany, Italy and Switzerland. The London–Bratislava overnight service takes just over 24 hours, but costs more than the cheapest budget flights. For timetable information visit: www.eurolines.com.

Within Slovakia: travelling by long-distance coach can work out cheaper and faster than the train, especially when a rail journey involves a change. Bus stations are usually conveniently sited in town centres and near rail stations, though the main Bratislava hub is in the suburbs. For timetable information visit: www.slovaklines.sk.

Local Public Transport

The whole of Slovakia is covered by a dense network of bus routes, serving even the remotest rural locations. However, timetabling is often determined by the needs of people commuting to and from work rather than those of holidaymakers, with, for

example, few services at weekends. The urban bus network is equally comprehensive, and in Bratislava and Košice is supplemented by trams. The normal procedure in cities is to purchase a ticket from a kiosk or ticket machine and cancel it once aboard the vehicle.

Taxis

Taxis are available in all towns and are generally reliable and not too expensive, though it is always worth checking the fare before starting your journey.

Car Hire

The principal international car-rental companies are represented in Slovakia at locations such as Bratislava and Košice airports. Significant savings are possible by hiring a vehicle from a local firm. Reliable operators include: Auto Danubius, Trnavská 39, 831 04 Bratislava; tel: 02 443 72 502; www.autotuzex.sk.

V

VISAS AND PASSPORTS

Citizens of EU countries may enter Slovakia with a valid identity card (or passport where applicable, as in the case of the UK) for a period up to 90 days (180 days in some cases). Other nationals may require a visa, though this is not the case for citizens of Australia, Canada, New Zealand and the US. Visas must be obtained from a Slovak embassy or consulate in advance of travel. Border controls were abolished for nationals of Schengen Area countries when Slovakia became a member, in 2008.

W

WEBSITES

General Information
• **www.heartofeurope.sk** (Keen US site, includes a list of 'famous Slovaks'.)
• **www.sacr.sk** (Slovak Tourist Authority site.)
• **www.slovakia.com**
• **www.bcsa.co.uk** (Information about the activities of the British Czech & Slovak Association, with links to other sites.)

Accommodation
• **www.travelguide.sk**

News
• **www.slovakspectator.sk** (Bratislava's weekly English-language newspaper.)
• **www.tasr.sk** (Weekly news in English.)
• **www.sri.sk** (News from Radio Slovakia International.)

Travel
• **www.vlak-bus.cz** (Efficient Czech-based website for rail and bus travel.)

Localities
The more popular cities and regions have websites in English, although they are of variable quality:
• **www.bkis.sk** (Very informative official Bratislava website.)
• **www.tatry.sk** (High Tatras)
If you are looking for information about individual localities, entering the place-name on a search engine usually produces a result, often, though not always, in English.

Finding a suitable place to stay in Slovakia has become steadily easier over the last few years, and in popular areas there is now a range of accommodation to suit most tastes. Elsewhere, particularly in the east of the country, choice is restricted, and standards are generally lower. Most Communist-era hotels have undergone full refurbishment, though a few have retained the atmosphere and less than forthcoming service of those times. The system of grading hotels with one to five stars gives only an approximate guide as to what to expect.

While room rates in Bratislava and the High Tatras approach Western European levels, elsewhere there are plenty of bargains to be had. Prices rise at times of high demand, which vary according to area. Bratislava can be cheaper in August, when business travel is virtually non-existent, and weekend deals can be found for most of the year. The Christmas/New Year period tends to be expensive everywhere. Mountain resorts charge their maximum rates during high summer and the winter sports season (normally Dec–Mar). Some of the best bargains are in private guesthouses (*penzión*) and private rooms (adver-tised as *ubytovania* or in German *Privat* or *Zimmer*), though standards are very variable.

Slovaks are happy campers, and there are campsites all over the country, often with chalets (*chata* or bungalow); rates are usually very affordable, but again, quality is variable.

Prices are posted in Slovak crowns and, frequently, in euros. Credit cards are accepted in establishments with any pretensions, but by no means everywhere. The minimal local tax charged is usually included in the bill, as is breakfast, but you will need to check the latter.

Banská Bystrica

Arcade

Námestie SNP 5, 974 01 Banská Bystrica; tel: 048 430 2111/4302 500; www.arcade.sk; €€

Charmingly located down one of the many ancient passageways leading off Banská Bystrica's main square, this sensitively modernised 16th-century building has been converted into a small hotel, and has to be *the* place to stay in this historic town.

Lux

Námestie slobody 2, 974 01 Banská Bystrica; tel: 048 4144 1415; www.hotellux.sk; €€

On the level ground just below the SNP Museum and town centre, this white high-rise slab was a Communist-era prestige project. It offers reliable accommodation and a wide range of facilities for its mostly business clientele.

Price based on two people sharing a double room for one night with breakfast:

€€€€	over 135 euros
€€€	90–135 euros
€€	45–90 euros
€	below 45 euros

Above from far left: exterior of Marrol's *(see p.108)*; coffee and cakes at the Thermia Palace *(see p.111)*.

Banská Štiavnica

Hotel Grand-Matej

Kammerhofská 5, 969 01 Banská Štiavnica; tel: 045 692 1231; €€

Comfortable, contemporary rooms in a fine old building just below the old town centre. Small wellness centre.

Penzión Prijemný Oddych

Starozámocká 3, 969 01 Banská Štiavnica; tel: 045 692 1301; www.prijemnyoddych; €

Immaculate private guesthouse set in an historic building close to the Old Castle in the upper part of town. Excellent value for money.

Bardejov and Bardejovské Kúpele

Bellevue Hotel

Mihaľov 2503, 085 01 Bardejov; tel: 054 472 8404; www.bellevuehotel.sk; €€

The most comfortable place to stay in and around Bardejov, the Bellevue is a new, contemporary-style hotel crowing a hilltop just outside the town, to which it is linked by the hotel minibus. Inviting rooms with good facilities, restaurant with gastronomic pretensions, barbecue pavilion, swimming pool, jacuzzi and tennis courts. Superb panorama from the terrace. The kitchen extractor fan disturbs the peace in some rooms.

Ozon

086 31 Bardejovské Kúpele; tel: 054 477 44 70; www.kupele-bj.sk; €€

With not far off 200 rooms, this 1970s concrete edifice is the largest establishment in Bardejov Spa, and a lingering notion of the old regime still clings to it despite extensive renovation. But it is comfortable enough, with a good range of facilities for its clientele, most of whom will be undergoing some form of spa treatment.

Penzión Semafor

Kellerova 13, 08 501 Bardejov; tel: 054 474 4433; www.penzionsemafor.sk; €

This small modern block of flats just a few steps from Bardejov's main square has been converted into apartments offering plain but tastefully furnished accommodation with a shared kitchen.

Bratislava

Hotel Devín

Riečna 4, 811 02 Bratislava; tel: 02 5998 5856; www.hoteldevin.sk; €€€–€€€€

Built in a restrained and still rather appealing Functionalist style in the 1950s, the Devín was for many years the city's only luxury hotel. It has maintained its reputation and has kept up to date with successive refurbishments, and offers every comfort and facility. The location is unsurpassable: the front rooms overlook the Danube, those at the rear have views of the castle.

Hotel Dukla

Dulovo námestie 1, 821 08 Bratislava; tel: 02 5596 8922; www.hoteldukla.sk; €€€–€€€€

Just about within walking distance of the Old Town, this large and rather faceless establishment in a Bratislava

inner suburb nevertheless has high standards of comfort and service and represents good value for money.

Ibis

Zámocká 38, 811 01 Bratislava; tel: 02 5929 2000; www.ibis.bratislava.sk; €€

Standardised, reliable accommodation from this branch of the international Ibis chain.

Hotel Kyjev

Rajská 2, 814 48 Bratislava; tel: 02 5964 1111; www.kyjev-hotel.sk; €€

The faceless multi-storey slab of the 'Kiev', built as a Socialist showpiece in the 1960s, looms over the eastern edge of the city centre. Refurbished rooms with great views (those without television are cheaper). Ideal for lovers of Communist chic. Good value.

Marrol's

Tobrucká 4, 811 02 Bratislava; tel: 02 5778 4600; www.hotel marrols.sk; €€€€

In a side street in the eastern part of the Old Town and opened in 2003, this medium-sized luxury establishment offers individually furnished rooms and attractive public spaces in an appealing retro style. It has been described as the best hotel in the whole country and is highly recommended. Gourmet Mediterranean restaurant.

Perugia

Zelená 5, 821 01 Bratislava; tel: 02 5443 1818; www.perugia.sk; €€€€

This attractive, highly recommended establishment is a comfortable place to stay in the heart of the New Town. Just 12 rooms. The attached pizza restaurant sometimes puts on live music.

Radisson SAS Carlton

Hviezdoslavovo námestie 3, 811 02 Bratislava; tel: 02 5939 0000; www.radissonsas.com; €€€€

Since its recent complete renovation, this legendary grand hotel has regained its position as a city institution. With a history going well back into the 19th century, it occupies a key position on Bratislava's most elegant square and provides every comfort.

Tatra

Námestie 1. mája 5, 811 06 Bratislava; tel: 02 5927 2111; www.hoteltatra.sk; €€€

This medium-sized establishment's chief asset is its location almost next door to the Presidential Palace, while its rooms are no more than adequate.

Turist

Ondavská 5, 820 05 Bratislava; tel: 02 5557 2789; www.turist.sk; €

With a guarded car park and only a short tram ride from the centre, the Turist offers basic accommodation

> Price based on two people sharing a double room for one night with breakfast:
>
> €€€€ over 135 euros
> €€€   90–135 euros
> €€   45–90 euros
> €   below 45 euros

with more than a whiff of the Communist era about it, but is quite satisfactory and excellent value.

Košice

Alessandria

Jiskrova 3, 040 01 Košice; tel: 055 622 5903; www.alessandria.sk; €€
A comfortable small hotel in a refurbished old building in a residential street about 10 minutes' walk from the station and the same distance from the northern end of the city centre.

Hotel Bristol

Orlia 3, 040 01 Košice; tel: 055 729 0077; www.hotelbristol.sk; €€€
Reckoned by many to be Košice's finest hotel, the Bristol is a medium-sized modern establishment sensitively inserted into the historic fabric of the city centre. All comforts and facilities.

Penzión Golden Royal

Vodná 8, 040 01 Košice; tel: 055 720 1011; www.goldenroyal.sk;
€€–€€€
In an historical city-centre building, this *penzión* provides its guests with four-star accommodation in an intimate setting at very reasonable rates.

Hotel Slávia

Hlavná 63, 040 01 Košice; tel: 055 622 4395; www.hotelslavia.sk; €€€
Occupying the same prominent Art Nouveau edifice on Košice's main square as the famous Slávia café, the hotel offers spacious rooms on its upper floors. A disadvantage of its central location in the city's pedestrian zone is the need to haul your luggage some distance from car or taxi.

Hotel Slovan

Hlavná 1, 040 01 Košice; tel: 055 622 7378; www.hotelslovan.sk; €€€
This establishment certainly lives up to its address ('no. 1 Main Street'). A multi-storey slab of a building, it is one of the landmarks of Communist-era Košice and still dominates the landscape at the southern end of the old city centre. Orientated towards the business traveller, it has been refurbished and offers decent accommodation (with fine views from the upper floors), as well as a bar that is one of the city's social centres and the 'Golden Prague' restaurant. There are plans to transform the Slovan into Košice's only five-star hotel; see website to check for updates.

Levoča

Hotel Barbakan

Košická 15, 054 01 Levoča; tel: 053 451 4310; www.barbakan.sk; €
In the heart of Levoča, close to one of the Old Town gates, the 'Barbican' is a small hotel in a medieval building offering very acceptable accommodation at reasonable rates. Its pleasant restaurant offers standard fare.

Hotel Satel

Námestie Majstra Pavla 55, 054 01 Levoča; tel: 053 451 2943-6; www.hotelsatel.com; €–€€
On Levoča's main square, this is one of the Old Town's finest buildings, a town mansion whose origins go back to the 14th century and which boasts a

superb galleried courtyard. Four-star accommodation in comfortable rooms with contemporary décor, some of them extremely spacious. Bar, recommended restaurant and atmospheric wine cellar.

Liptov

Defined to the south by the long ridge of the Low Tatra mountains, the Liptov region straddles the routeways leading from western Slovakia to the High Tatras. The main town is Liptovský Mikuláš, but the most attractive places to stay are in the valleys leading into the mountains, from where there is easy access to the heights.

Hotel Grand

032 51 Jasná, Demänovská Dolina; tel: 044 559 1441-3; www.grandjasna.sk; €€

The Demänovská valley is famed for its caves (called, like the valley itself, Demänovské jaskyne), the most visited in the country, as well as for its very extensive ski facilities on the slopes of the Low Tatras. The Grand is a large but not monolithic modern building offering the best accommodation in the area with a good range of facilities and a decent restaurant.

Price based on two people sharing a double room for one night with breakfast:

€€€€	over 135 euros
€€€	90–135 euros
€€	45–90 euros
€	below 45 euros

Liptovský dvor

Jánska dolina 438, 032 03 Liptovský Ján; tel: 044 520 7500; www.liptovskydvor.sk; €€€€

Halfway along the Janská valley leading into the heart of the Low Tatras national park, this recently constructed establishment consists of a group of traditionally built chalets arranged as a 'village' and centred on a gourmet restaurant and main building with reception and spacious but cosy lounge. Built with great attention to detail, the charming and comfortable chalets accommodate four to six people. There are plenty of sporting and recreational facilities including a nearby ski lift.

Martin

Hotel Turiec

A Sokolíka 2, 036 01 Martin; tel: 043 422 1017-9; www.hotel-turiec.sk; €–€€

Dating back to the 1960s, Martin's most prominent hotel is a typical Communist-era concrete block, but has undergone a fairly complete makeover. Its central location makes it the best choice hereabouts.

Medzilaborce

Penzión Andy

Andyho Warhola 121, 068 01 Medzilaborce; tel: 057 732 1640; www.penzionandy.sk; €

Lacking the pretension of Medzilaborce's Eurohotel just up the road, this modest guesthouse and café is probably the best place to stay in what is something of a desert as far as accommodation is concerned.

Piešťany

The Château

Kaštiel Šalgovce, 956 06 Šalgovce; tel: 038 539 5155; www.the chateau.sk; €€€–€€€€

From the centre of Piešťany, a ten-minute drive over the wooded hills leads to this exquisite manor house in the centre of the village of Šalgovce. The loving restoration of this Baroque jewel has been carried out by an enterprising British couple, whose sometimes heroic efforts have been featured in a series of television programmes. The interiors have been furnished lavishly and with great attention to detail. Equivalent care is taken with the preparation and presentation of fine food, served in the domed chapel or on the terrace with country views.

Thermia Palace

Kúpeľný ostrov, 921 29 Piešťany; tel: 033 775 7733; www.spapiestany.sk; €€€€

Restored to its former glory by a thoroughgoing refurbishment in 2006 and now the country's first five-star hotel, the Art Nouveau grande dame of Slovakia's most prestigious spa town offers its guests luxurious accommodation and every possible facility. The centrepiece of its splendid restaurant is a painting by Alfons Mucha, presented to the hotel by the artist in thanks for his daughter's successful cure here.

Above from far left: guests at the Thermia Palace can use a golf course close to the hotel; in the Grand Restaurant at the Thermia Palace is an Art Nouveau painting *(detail above)* by Moravian-born Alfons Mucha, who donated it to the spa as a gift for curing his daughter.

Left: smart exterior of The Château.

Rožňava

Čierny Orol

Námestie Baníkov 17, 048 01
Rožňava; tel: 058 732 81 86;
www.ciernyorol.sk; €

In a carefully adapted historic building
on Rožňava's vast central square, the
hotel has decently furnished accommodation, a restaurant, cellar bar and
an outdoor terrace.

Spišská Kapitula

Kolpingov dom

Spišská Kapitula 15, Spišské
Podhradie; tel: 053 450 2111;
www.hotelkolping.sk; €€

A rare opportunity to stay in the very
heart of the Spiš country, the Kolping
House occupies one of the historic
buildings in this unique little ecclesiastical city. Atmospheric, comfortable, if
somewhat sombre, rooms – including
the Bishop's Apartment – and a decent
restaurant and wine cellar.

Tatra Mountains

AquaCity Poprad

Športová 1397/1, 058 01 Poprad; tel:
052 785 1111; www.aquacity.sk; €€€

An extraordinary complex of thermal
pools and other health and wellness
facilities (including frightening-
sounding cryotherapy, during which
you are exposed to a temperature of
−120°C/−184°F) has sprung up at the
foot of the Tatras in the otherwise
undistinguished town of Poprad. With
two hotels and an array of restaurants
and bars, it makes an excellent base
from which to explore the region.

Grand Hotel

062 01 Starý Smokovec; tel: 052
478 0000; www.grandhotel.sk; €€€

This splendid Edwardian edifice has
dominated the centre of the little mountain resort of Starý Smokovec since it
was built at the beginning of the 20th
century. It maintains its reputation for
luxurious living in a nostalgic setting.

Liečebný dom Solisko

Štrbské Pleso 27, 059 85 Štrbské
Pleso; tel: 052 478 0722;
www.solisko.sk; €€€

This beautifully refurbished spa hotel
stands right by the lakeshore in
Štrbské Pleso and offers its guests
every comfort as well as the possibility
of invigorating treatments.

Hotel Patria

Štrbské Pleso; tel: 052 449 2591-5;
www.hotelpatria.sk; €€

A Communist-era showpiece, with a
distinctive pointed outline supposedly
harmonising with its mountain setting,
the 300-bed Patria in Štrbské Pleso is
one of the most prominent features in
the landscape around this highland
resort. Comfortable rooms and apartments, extraordinarily lavish public
spaces and most of the facilities to be
expected in a four-star establishment.

Hotel Sobota

Kežmarská 988/15, Spišská Sobota,
058 01 Poprad; tel: 052 466 3121;
www.hotelsobota.sk; €€

Charmingly located on the river bank
just below the medieval township of
Spišská Sobota, this recently built small

hotel is an attractive and comfortable alternative to the many guesthouses and pensions in the Old Town. Its quiet, semi-rural location commends it to business travellers visiting the industrial city of Poprad, of which Spišská Sobota is nominally a part, but which in spirit is a world away.

Terchová

Hotel Boboty

013 06 Terchová; tel: 041 569 5228; www.hotelboboty.sk; €€

A superior Communist-era establishment, much improved by its more recent owners, making the most of its prominent position on a sunny, south-facing slope. Most of the rooms have stupendous views of the mountains, as do the light and airy bar, café and restaurant. To get there, drive south from Terchová along the Vrátna valley and turn left towards Štefanová, then left again up the drive leading to the hotel.

Gavurky

Sv. Martina 1400, 013 06 Terchová; tel: 041 500 3502-3; www.hotelgavurky.sk; €

A modern, medium-sized hotel with restaurant on the eastern outskirts of Terchová mountain resort in the Malá Fatra national park.

Trenčianske Teplice

Penzión Baske

17 novembra 23; Trenčianske Teplice; tel 032 655 34 28; www.penzionbaske.sk; €€

Stay in style in one of the original ornate 19th-century villas that embellish this spa town. Fully refurbished with exceptional care in 2004, this luxurious little establishment is noted for its comfort and its welcoming staff.

Parkhotel na Baračke

Baračka 87, Trenčianske Teplice; tel: 032 655 6868; www.palacehotels.sk; €€

Situated in an attractive leafy setting, this small establishment has won accolades including being placed among the country's top 10 hotels. It offers a range of spa treatments and has a highly recommended restaurant.

Žilina

Grand

Sladkovičova 1, 01 001 Žilina; tel: 041 562 6809; www.hotelgrand.sk; €€

Opened in 1910, this medium-sized, recently refurbished establishment is conveniently located right in the centre of town at the beginning of a street leading off the northwest corner of Žilina's arcaded main square. The hotel's amenities include a restaurant, café, nightclub and wellness centre; there are also parking facilities, which is a definite advantage given the town-centre location.

Price based on two people sharing a double room for one night with breakfast:

€€€€	over 135 euros
€€€	90–135 euros
€€	45–90 euros
€	below 45 euros

The list below features our top choices, especially for evening dining, across the country. In addition to conventional restaurants *(reštaurácia)*, eating establishments include: wine cellars *(vináreň)*, which are similar but may stay open longer and offer a wider choice of wine; pubs *(piváreň)*; and rustic *koliba* and *salaš*, both variations on the traditional shepherd's hut, serving traditional dishes in a cosy setting.

There are a few points of etiquette to note when eating out in Slovakia. If a restaurant is crowded, it is normal to share a table with fellow-diners, though not before checking *Je tu volno?* (literally: 'is it free?'). When your neighbours are served with their meal it is polite to wish them *dobrou chut'!* (equivalent of 'bon appétit'!), and also to say *dovidenia* ('goodbye') when one or other of you leave.

Note that smoking is not banned in restaurants in Slovakia. Many Slovaks remain enthusiastic smokers, placing a lighter and an open pack of cigarettes as well as a mobile by their place setting as they sit down at a table. If smoke bothers you, check whether your chosen restaurant is smoke-free or at least has a non-smoking section.

Finally, note also that service is normally included in the price of a

restaurant meal, though it is customary to make up the amount you give to the nearest round number. Be aware that a charge is made in some establishments for what you might expect to be complimentary appetisers, as well as for such items as rolls and butter.

Banská Bystrica

Červený rak

Námestie SNP 13; tel: 048 472 1501/ 048 415 38 82; www.cervenyrak.sk; €€–€€€

With a prime position on the town's main square, the capacious 'Red Lobster' offers a wide choice of eating and drinking; there is a conventional restaurant (where goose is a speciality), a barrel-vaulted 'beer house' with meals to match, and a rustic *koliba* with traditional Slovak fare. In summer you can sit in the enclosed courtyard or see and be seen on the square itself.

Reštaurácia Bašta

Kapitulská 23; tel: 048 412 6281; www.bastabb.sk; €€

In the park laid out around the SNP Museum, the 'Bastion' forms part of the town fortifications. Its thick walls provide a cool ambience in summer for a ground-floor snack bar, a stylish first-floor café with music and dancing, and an attractive top-floor smoke-free restaurant serving standard Slovak fare.

Slovenská reštaurácia

Horná 39; tel: 048 415 5036; €

A short walk from the main square, this many-roomed basement establishment offers an international menu as

well as specialities based on grandma's traditional Slovakian recipes.

Steak House

Námestie Štefana Moyzesa 2; tel: 048 412 3091; www.steakhouse-bb.sk; €€

Just up from the main square, the Steak House lives up to its name with a wide range of grilled meats and a tasty goulash. It is considered by some to be the best restaurant in town.

Bratislava

Chez David

Zámocká 13; tel: 02 5441 3824; www.chezdavid.sk; €€

Below the castle, this kosher establishment has revived Bratislava's venerable Jewish culinary traditions.

Francúzská reštaurácia

Hotel Devín, Riečna 4; tel: 02 5998 5202; www.hoteldevin.sk; €€€€

The classically elegant French Restaurant of the waterfront Hotel Devín maintains its reputation as one of the city's leading gourmet establishments. Fresh, seasonally varied ingredients go into its French, international and Slovak dishes, and there is a vast array of local and imported wines.

Gazdovský Dvor

Hotel Perugia, Zelená 5; tel: 02 5443 1818; www.perugia.sk; €€€

One of the best places in Bratislava to sample the tasty delights of the cuisine of neighbouring Hungary, notably *halaslé*, fiery fish soup with more than a dash of paprika.

Kaffé Mayer

Hlavné námestie 4; tel: 02 5441 1741; €

Kaffé Mayer looks across the main square towards its rival, the Roland *(see p.33)*, and is the epitome of the old-style Central European café, with exactly the right kind of coffee and cakes as well as the atmosphere.

Le Monde

Rybárska brána 8, Hviezdoslavovo námestie; tel: 02 5441 5411; www.lemonde.sk; €€€€

Famous for its quintet of gourmet restaurants in Prague, the Kampa Group is well represented in Bratislava by this refined establishment located opposite the National Theatre. Dishes are drawn from a global repertoire, and there is an extensive wine list.

Matyšák

Pražská 15; tel: 020 2063 4001; €€

This renowned wine restaurant is run by a leading family of vintners from

Above from far left: dining room at Le Monde; bottles at a winery in the Little Carpathians.

Below: alfresco dining on Bratislava's tree-lined Hviez-doslavovo námestie *(see p.29)*, near the Slovak National Theatre.

the Little Carpathians. It offers local specialities, rustic ambience and live folk music on some evenings. It is located outside the old centre, close to the main station.

Slovak Pub

Obchodná 62; tel: 02 5292 6367; www.slovakpub.sk; €

Don't be put off by the name – this is in fact an admirable venture by an enterprising individual aiming to provide decent ordinary food and drink at reasonable prices. It's more of a student hang-out than a tourist trap, with an incredible variety of interiors, including a real log-cabin brought here all the way from the far-off Orava district in the north of the country. There's a wide range of draught beers, including the house's own brew, 'Dobré pifko'.

Slovenská Reštaurácia

Hviezdoslavovo námestie 20; tel: 02 5441 6442; www.slovrest.sk; €€€

Long-established restaurant with an outdoor terrace overlooking the action on this attractive square, plus a tastefully decorated, folksy interior. Official visitors from abroad are often brought here, since the restaurant has suc-

ceeded in maintaining its reputation for serving traditional Slovak dishes with more than a touch of style.

Trafená Hus

Šafárikovo námestie 7; tel: 02 5292 5473; www.trafenahus.sk; €€

The 'Shot Goose' is related to a range of similar, very successful establishments in Prague, operated by the Staropramen brewery group, and aimed at the discerning young. The place is airy and offers good value for money. There's a wide choice of tempting, (fairly) healthy dishes and snacks, and the drinks are served by expert bar staff.

UFO watch.taste.groove

Nový most; tel: 02 6252 0300; www.u-f-o.sk; €€€€

Often compared to an Unidentified Flying Object, the disc-shaped platform high above the futuristic New Bridge (Nový most) houses the country's most unusual restaurant. Reopened in 2005, it matches the superlative panorama of river and city with outstanding fusion cuisine, albeit at a price.

Veža

Cesta na Kamzík 14, Bratislava Koliba; tel: 02 4446 2774; www.veza.sk; €€€

The revolving restaurant incorporated into the television tower in the hills above Bratislava offers a range of decent international dishes, but the real attraction is the ever-changing panorama, which in fine conditions

> Price guide for a main course and glass of house wine, with service included:
> €€€€   18 euros and above
>   (545SK and above)
> €€€   11–18 euros (335–545SK)
> €€   7–11 euros (212–335SK)
> €   below 7 euros (212SK)

extends over four countries (Hungary, Austria, the Czech Republic and, of course, Slovakia).

Above from far left: in a traditional bar; elegantly set table at the Radisson SAS Carlton *(see p.108)*.

Košice

12 apoštolov

Kováčska 51; tel: 055 729 5104; www.12apostolov.sk; €€–€€€

Installed in an elegant century-old building in a street that runs parallel to the main square, the 'Twelve Apostles' is one of Košice's leading restaurants, with international and Slovak dishes on its menu.

Ajvega

Orlia 10; tel: 055 622 0452; €

Located one street away from Košice's main square, this well-established vegetarian restaurant is a welcome find in this meat-craving country. Carnivores are also catered for with a small number of meat dishes. There's a characterful interior and an outside terrace in summer.

Golden Royal

Vodná 8; tel: 055 720 1011; www.goldenroyal.sk; €€

Part of the highly rated pension of the same name, this restaurant has gained much acclaim for its charming winter garden atmosphere, its notable wine list and its typical Slovak or Hungarian daily specials at good prices.

Le Colonial

Hlavná 8; tel: 055 729 6126; €€

Reached through a courtyard from the main square, Le Colonial lives up to its name with a stylish interior and individual furnishings evoking the Mediterranean and North Africa. The international menu with many original offerings tempts the city's in-crowd.

Plzeňská hospoda

Biela 3; tel: 055 622 0402; €

An outpost of Bohemian beer culture in far eastern Slovakia, the city centre 'Pilsen Pub' conjures up the spirit of the Good Soldier Švejk with hearty food and excellent ale.

Uhorský dvor

Bočná 10; tel: 055 728 8493; www.uhorskydvor.sk; €€

Conveniently located one street west of Košice's main square, and saving you the trouble of crossing the nearby border, the 'Hungarian Court' with its outdoor terrace and wine cellar serves typical specialities of the tasty and distinctive Magyar cuisine, often to the accompaniment of 'Gypsy' music.

Zlatá Praha

Hotel Slovan, Hlavná 1; tel: 055 622 7378; www.hotelslovan.sk; €€–€€€

The 'Golden Prague' restaurant of the Hotel Slovan exudes the stiff atmosphere of Communist times, but the Slovak and international dishes are well prepared and the service is professional.

Liptov

Defined to the south by the long ridge of the Low Tatra mountains, the Liptov region straddles the routeways leading from western Slovakia to the High Tatras. The main town is Liptovský Mikuláš, but the most attractive places to stay are in the valleys leading into the mountains, from where there is easy access to the heights.

Hotel Tri Studničky

032 51 Jasná, Demänovská dolina 5; tel: 044 547 8000; www.tristudnicky.sk; €€€

The award-winning, modern chalet-type 'Three Springs' has a restaurant to match, commanded by a celebrity chef who has starred in his own television programme. Inventive international dishes served with flair. Outdoor dining on the terrace in summer.

Liptovský dvor

032 03 Liptovský Ján, Jánska dolina 438; tel: 044 520 7500; www.liptovskydvor.sk; €€€

Gourmet meals are served with a flourish by costumed staff in this

Right: a refreshing Slovak beer *(pivo)*.

contemporary version of a timber mountain hut, part of a hotel 'village' in a valley running into the Low Tatra mountains. Dishes include tempting vegetarian options, but game and fish are the main specialities. Conveniently located near the Liptovský Ján interchange on the motorway leading to the High Tatras.

Tatra Mountains

Grand Hotel Praha

059 60 Tatranská Lomnica, Vysoké Tatry; tel: 052 446 7941; www.ghpraha.sk; €€–€€€

Like the Grand in Jasná *(see p.110)*, the Praha in the neighbouring mountain resort of Tatranská Lomnica is one of the country's great luxury hotels from the golden age of early 20th-century tourism, and has a gourmet restaurant to match.

Koliba Patria

Štrbské Pleso; tel: 052 449 2591; www.hotelpatria.sk; €€

Overlooking the lake shore at Štrbské Pleso, this is a contemporary version of the traditional Slovak *koliba,* with elaborate décor including a farm cart dangling from the ceiling. Superior Slovak food and a wonderful view if you manage to get a window seat.

Penzión Sabato

Sobotské námestie 1730/6, Spišská Sobota, 058 01 Poprad; tel: 052 776 9589; www.sabato.sk; €€–€€€

One of several guesthouses on the perfectly preserved square of the tiny town of Spišská Sobota at the foot of the Tatra mountains, this delightful 17th-century building also houses a rather characterful restaurant with themed interiors (blacksmith's, baker's, burgher's). The food is of an exceptionally high standard with a number of original recipes.

Žilina

Rybárska Bašta

Ulice osloboditeľov 12, Rajecké Teplice; tel: 041 549 4030; €€

Only 12km (7 miles) south of Žilina, Rajecké Teplice is a well-kept little spa town. This restaurant, the 'Fishermen's Bastion', is on an island in a landscaped lake, and, appropriately, offers fishy specialities. It belongs to the adjacent ostentatiously luxurious Aphrodite spa hotel, which has its own restaurant.

Voyage Voyage

Mariánske námestie 191; tel: 041 564 0230; www.voyagevoyage.sk; €

This popular, trendy café-restaurant on the main square of Žilina, the regional capital, is almost always busy, not least on Friday and Saturday evenings, when it is open until 2am. There is an extensive menu and drinks list, with the best bargains at lunchtime, when there is a choice of daily specialities.

Price guide for a main course and glass of house wine, with service included:

€€€€	18 euros and above (545SK and above)
€€€	11–18 euros (335–545SK)
€€	7–11 euros (212–335SK)
€	below 7 euros (212SK)

INSIGHT CITY GUIDES

The Guides That Are Streets Ahead

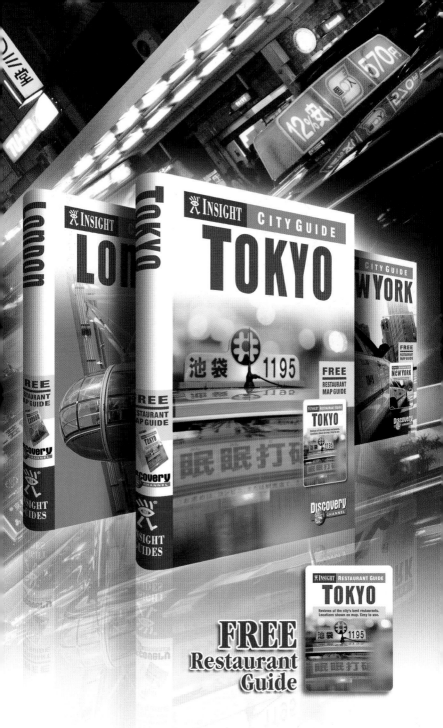

*Insight Guides to every major country
are also available*

www.insightguides.com

CREDITS

Insight Step by Step Slovakia
Written by: Mike Ivory
Series Editor: Clare Peel
Cartography Editors: Zoë Goodwin and James Macdonald
Picture Manager: Steven Lawrence
Art Editor: Ian Spick
Production: Kenneth Chan
Photography: All Images © APA/Anna Mockford and Nick Bonetti except:
Alamy 22–3, 41, 48T, 55T, 60T, 76B, 77T; APA/Justin Hannaford 6MR, 6BL, 7BR, 16B, 21TR, 48M, 49T, 52TL, 52B, 56TL, 66T, 78MT, 78MB, 78B, 80T, 81T, 89TL, 89B, 94, 95, 98–9, 101, 103, 115T; APA/Corrie Wingate 14TR; Bridgeman 24TL; Corbis 25TR; Istockphoto 10B, 10TL, 12B, 13TL, 17TL, 19TR, 20–1, 20TL, 21B, 28TL, 55B, 62B, 96, 100, 118B; Leonardo 108, 109, 117; Photolibrary 59B; Thermia Piestany 17B, 42, 110, 111T, 107, 118T.

Cover: main image: Photolibrary; bottom left: Bon Appetit/Alamy; bottom right: APA/Anna Mockford and Nick Bonetti.

Printed by: Insight Print Services (Pte) Ltd, 38 Joo Koon Road, Singapore 628990

First Edition 2009

CONTACTING THE EDITORS

We would appreciate it if readers would alert us to errors or outdated information by writing to us at insight@apaguide.co.uk or APA Publications, PO Box 7910, London SE1 1WE, UK.

www.insightguides.com

DISTRIBUTION

Worldwide
APA Publications GmbH & Co. Verlag KG
(Singapore branch), 38 Joo Koon Road,
Singapore 628990
Tel: (65) 6865 1600
Fax: (65) 6861 6438

UK and Ireland
GeoCenter International Ltd
Meridian House, Churchill Way West,
Basingstoke, Hampshire, RG21 6YR
Tel: (44) 01256 817 987
Fax: (44) 01256 817 988

United States
Langenscheidt Publishers, **Inc.**
36–36 33rd Street, 4th Floor,
Long Island City, NY 11106
Tel: (1) 718 784 0055
Fax: (1) 718 784 0640

Australia
Universal Publishers
1 Waterloo Road, Macquarie Park, NSW 2113
Tel: (61) 2 9857 3700
Fax: (61) 2 9888 9074

New Zealand
Hema Maps New Zealand Ltd (HNZ)
Unit D, 24 Ra ORA Drive,
East Tamaki, Auckland
Tel: (64) 9 273 6459
Fax: (64) 9 273 6479

RESTAURANT INDEX

HOTEL INDEX

INDEX

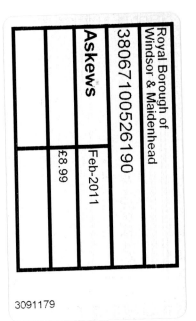

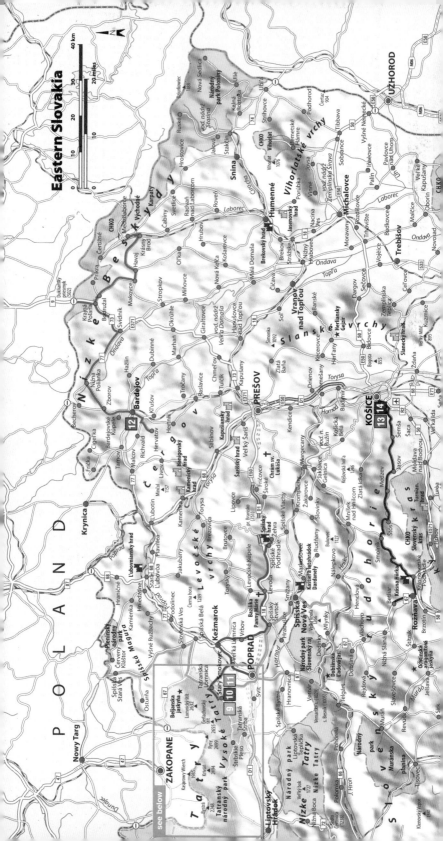